I0441364

IMPACT ON AMERICAN HIGHER EDUCATION

The Prevalence of the "Eating Disorder Not Otherwise Specified" (EDNOS) Category with Examination of the "Eating Disorder Bodybuilding Type" (EDBT) Category among Division I-A Varsity Male Student-Athletes

by

Robert Louis Suglia, Jr., Ph.D.

A dissertation submitted to the State University of New York at Buffalo, Department of Educational Leadership and Policy for the degree of Doctorate of Philosophy.

ISBN: 1441450017
EAN-13:   9781441450012

Acknowledgments

In the past two years I have spent researching and writing on a personal topic that was once private and hidden, I have found this dissertation develop into an extension of myself. What began as an attempt to "solve" my eating disorder has become an outlet to express ambiguous feelings with the clarity of the written word.

As the final step this publication, it is with a strong sense of gratitude that I acknowledge Dr. Bill Barba. I have seen his concern and compassion change the lives of my peers; and although he may not realize the impact he has made, we have.

What was to be a short work-related meeting during the summer of 2001 turned into an impromptu "counseling session" as Dr. Barba spoke about the potential he saw in me. Admittedly, I remember wondering how he was able to see with such clarity what I have always successfully hidden. After our meeting, I decided to apply to the university's doctoral program. This single interaction has been a defining moment that stays with me as I strive to become a more authentic person.

I am also grateful for the kindness of Dr. Henry Durand and Dr. LeAdelle Phelps. Dr. Durand's style of teaching brought humor to my statistic classes – a part of the program that I was most fearful of and caused a two year delay in my decision to apply. Ironically, his classes were the most enjoyable of all my coursework as Dr. Durand's willingness to provide additional help allowed me to overcome a lifelong fear of math. Dr. Phelps kindness has come in the way of support – in spending time with me over her academic break to form my research questions and help me run the proper statistical tests to her thoughtful feedback on my chapters, writing style, and reinforcing the importance of the dissertation's topic.

As my faculty committee has given me tremendous support, the most valuable inspiration has come from my sister Donna. During my life, she has taken our relationship beyond that of sister and brother. She has been a "second mother" and a best friend to me. In the past year, I have seen courage, strength, and determination in her humble approach to a diagnosis of breast cancer. Her husband Bob has been my most influential male role-model. For over 16-years, I continue to admire the manner in which he treats and cares for others, finding the good in all. Bob has taught me what is truly important in life by always putting his family first and that true masculinity comes from what is inside and one conducts themselves - not their outward physical appearance. Their daughters, Jessie Rose and Lily, although only eight and six years-old, have unexpectedly given me a great deal of freedom from my struggles with food and exercise. In moving to Colorado and being accepted into their family, I have come to love both of them more than I knew was possible. My only hope is for them to never understand the struggle of an eating disorder and to one day realize how happy they have made me and how they have changed my life.

Table of Contents

FIGURES

APPENDIX

Abstract

With the majority of eating disorder research and literature centered on the female perspective, intertwined myths and stigmas have been woven into the fabric of the American culture. Scholarship on anorexia and bulimia holds a clear position of dominance as the third and final clinical eating disorder category is often ignored. The eating disorder "not otherwise specified" (EDNOS) category is the most frequently prescribed eating disorder, is suspected to hold a gender-neutral prevalence rate, and has been detected with high rates of occurrences in male athlete populations. Even with the promise of a greater understanding of the disease and the dynamic of ill males, the "not otherwise specified" category remains understudied and is often excluded from research and literature. This neglect permits a continuation of existing misperceptions to breed a social ignorance, uncertainty, and embarrassment for the overlooked male population suffering with eating disorders; abandoned in a culture that does not socially and most often does not medically recognize their disease. The further study on the unique relationship among the "not otherwise specified" category, males, and college athletics will contribute to eating disorder etiology. Advancement in this area can lead to a more truthful account of ill males and the understanding that the disease is equally severe among both genders. As forthcoming studies continue to agree with the gender commonalities of predisposing traits, the stigmatic view of males with eating disorders may begin to lose credibility.

CHAPTER I: INTRODUCTION

Context of the Problem

Eating disorders are a significant American health issue worthy of empirical attention on both genders. As articulated in the review of literature that considered over 250 scholarly articles and studies, pathogenic and maladaptive eating and exercising behaviors occur in masses within the college and university environment.

Although most of these behaviors do not meet the APA's fourth edition of the Diagnostic and Statistical Manual (DSM-IV) criteria for anorexia or bulimia, some will meet the eating disorder "not otherwise specified" (EDNOS) standards. With the college athletic environment referred to as a "breeding ground" for eating disorders and EDNOS' high rate of prevalence with individual and social implications equal to anorexia and bulimia, the bearing of responsibility will in part befall on higher education. This study will assist colleges and universities to achieve a better understanding of their male student- athletes so institutions may be better equipped programmatically to implement gender-neutral preventative and intervening services.

While eating disorders are an assumed female affliction, the disease's prevalence in males has grown to an undetermined level. Considering the standard estimate that males account for 10% of all eating disorder cases in America, hundreds of thousands males are ill in a culture that does not recognize their illness socially or medically (APA, 1994). Still, this conservative estimate of 10% renders eating disorders as a significant health issue for American males; yet this approximation does not account for the large portion of males that are commonly unidentified and misdiagnosed. This truth is disheartening while considering occurrences of eating disorders are proven to be at their highest in the post-secondary environment and among competitive athletes. Thus, a male participating in competitive college athlete assumes the highest risk (most vulnerable) for developing an eating disorder. Unfortunately, both of these risk factors (the college environment and competitive athletics) only further hinder the innate difficulty of recognizing an eating disorder in males – for the college athletic environment regularly and openly promotes and accepts eating disorder behaviors and symptoms. Even among physicians, the flawed ability to detect this disease in males is due in part from the popular belief that eating disorders are a female affliction causing medical professionals to hold a lesser degree of suspicion among their male patients.

Even with these long-held societal beliefs, there are indications that these myths are changing. The considerable growth of America's fitness culture has modernized the ideal male physique, causing a deepened distress for men and their body image. This concern among males is particularly rampant in the culture of collegiate sports since physique and athletic success is linked to the athlete's perceived degree of masculinity. To advance the etiology and scholarship of males and eating disorders, further research is needed on the flawed relationship with food and exercise used by males to define his need for success in the realm of sports.

Purpose of the Study

Recognizing the deficiencies in eating disorder literature and research, this study is designed to examine the aspects of eating disorder scholarship that has promising, but understudied results. Following this objective, the study has controlled for all three clinical eating disorders (anorexia, bulimia, EDNOS) along with Gruber and Pope's 2000 proposed eating disorder "bodybuilding type" (EDBT) category that is believed to be highly prevalent among highly competitive male athletes. This study has an exclusive male sample and considers a wide-range of varsity sports that college males inhabit - not just the sports that are often included in similar studies based on their proven history of high eating disorder prevalence (e.g., wrestling). The exploration of these non-traditional areas will separate this study from the majority of existing eating disorder research and their unintended exclusionary biases.

This study examines if a sample of Division I-A male varsity athletes competing in the Mid-American Conference (MAC) yield an eating disorder "not otherwise specified" prevalence rate that exceeds the national male eating disorder statistic of 10%. The EDNOS classification is the third and final clinical eating disorder category adopted by the APA in 1994. EDNOS' origin (the sub-clinical term "atypical") was included in the APA's DSM-III in 1980. Anorexia and bulimia were the first two categories recognized by the APA, and were introduced in medial essays in as early as 1859 and 1976 respectively.

According to the DSM-IV (a classification system that provides empirically based, clear definitions of all recognized mental disorders) an EDNOS diagnosis is given when an individual engages in abnormal eating, yet some of the criteria for anorexia or bulimia remains unmet. EDNOS is assigned two criteria as anorexia or bulimia symptoms are "below the diagnostic threshold for one of the specific disorders or when there is an atypical or mixed presentation" (APA, 2004, p. 4).

From the narrow scope of studies that have included EDNOS in their methodology, strikingly high EDNOS prevalence rates were found: 65% (Black, Larkin, Coster, Leverenz, & Abood, 2003), 50% (Ricca, Mannucci & Mezzani, 2001); and

Mitchell, 1986), 43.8% (Button, 2005), 32% (Carlat, Camargo, &

Herzog, 1997). Although EDNOS is often excluded from eating

disorder research, the casual term of "disordered eating" has

come to identify subjects with a mixture or sub-threshold

anorexia or bulimia behaviors. Even though these two criteria

define the "not otherwise specified" category, researchers often

do not test this population for EDNOS and label them has having

disordered eating behaviors. It is likely that populations

identified with disordered eating actually have a clinical eating

disorder of EDNOS. Within some of these studies, a disorder

eating prevalence rate was produced that is equivalent to the

above studies that controlled for EDNOS: 61% Mintz and Bentz,

1986), 46% (Engel, Johnson, Powers, Crosby, Wonderlick,

Wottrock, & Mitchell, 2003), and 22% (Garman, Hayduk, Crider,

& Hodel (2004).

Even with these landmark rates of occurrences, this

clinical category is repeatedly excluded from studies as

researchers continue to solely control for the popular categories

of anorexia and bulimia. In doing so, researches have essentially predetermined a negligible prevalence rate among males. Even if the male population meets the criteria for EDNOS, they will most often evade the criteria for anorexia and bulimia. By obtaining results similar to studies that included EDNOS, further credibility may be added to those advocating the redirection of eating disorder research to regularly include the often-ignored EDNOS category. The secondary purpose of this study is to establish a prevalence rate for Gruber and Pope's (2000) eating disorder "bodybuilding type" (EDBT) category – a promising category whose proposed criteria is yet to be tested. With these intentions, this study is heavily reliant on the sample meeting the EDNOS criteria. If parallels emerge, it is hoped that the validity of eating disorder research with the intent of measuring the disease's prevalence will become dependent on including the EDNOS category.

Research Questions

Decades of research has established inherent or acquired personality characteristics of an athlete as deeply related to eating disorder behaviors and development. This scope of research has also proven that eating disorders occur more frequently in college and athletics than in those not attending a post-secondary institution or uninvolved in a structured sport program. The EDNOS and EDBT categories are the most favorable to the eating and exercise behaviors that both athletes and males frequently and openly display without due regard. Consequently, three research questions will be explored:

1. Among male varsity student-athletes who compete in the Mid-American Conference, what is the presence of anorexia and bulimia as defined by the American Psychiatric Association (2004) and EDBT as determined by Gruber and Pope's 2000 research?

2. Among male varsity student-athletes who compete in the Mid-American Conference, will the EDNOS category be the most common clinical eating disorder by exceeding the sample's occurrences of anorexia and bulimia?

3. Among male varsity student-athletes who compete in the Mid-American Conference, will the sample's sport be correlated to the presence of anorexia, bulimia, EDNOS, or EDBT?

Conceptualized Variables

Independent Variable (Conceptualized)

Male Varsity Sport Team: Will be defined as the eleven varsity sports that are exclusive to males and represented in some or all of the twelve MAC institutions (baseball, basketball, combined track, football, golf, ice hockey, soccer, swimming or diving, tennis, volleyball, and wrestling). A varsity team is defined as the principal team representing the institution in organized sport competitions, as it is distinctly different in culture and membership from a club or recreational team.

Dependent Variables (Conceptualized)

Presence of Anorexia Nervosa: Will be defined as the total number of occurrences of the anorexia category as self-reported by the student-athletes in questions #11-13 of the survey.

Presence of Bulimia Nervosa: Will be defined as the total number of occurrences of the bulimia category as self-reported by the student-athletes in questions #14-17 in the survey.

Presence of EDNOS: Will be defined as the total number of occurrences of the EDNOS category derived from the student-athletes' self-reported responses of survey question numbers five through 17.

Presence of EDBT: Will be defined as the total number of occurrences of the EDBT category as self-reported by the student-athletes in questions #5-10 the survey.

Definition of Terms

American Psychological Association (APA): A professional

organization representing American psychology to advance

psychology as a science and profession and as a means of

promoting health, education, and human welfare.

Anorexia Nervosa (Anorexia): "The essential features of

Anorexia Nervosa are that the individual refuses to maintain a

minimally normal body weight, is intensely afraid of gaining

weight, and exhibits a significant disturbance in the perception

of the shape or size of his or her body" (APA, 2004, p. 583).

Anorexia Nervosa Diagnostic Criteria (APA, 2004, p. 589):

1. Refusal to maintain body weight at or above a minimally
   normal weight for age and height (e.g., weight loss
   leading to maintenance of body weight less than 85% of
   that expected; or failure to make expected weight gain
   during period of growth, leading to body weight less
   than 85% of that expected).
2. Intense fear of gaining weight or becoming fat, even
   though underweight.
3. Disturbance in the way in which one's body weight or
   shape is experienced, undue influence of body weight

or shape on self-evaluation, or denial of the seriousness of the current low body weight.

4. In post menarcheal females the absence of at least three consecutive menstrual cycles. [Note: The criteria will be removed from the questionnaire as the study has a male sample].

Bulimia Nervosa (Bulimia): "The essential features of Bulimia

Nervosa are binge eating and inappropriate compensatory

behaviors to prevent weight gain. In addition, the self

evaluation of individuals with Bulimia Nervosa is excessively

influenced by body weight or shape" (APA, 2004, p. 589).

Bulimia Nervosa Diagnostic Criteria (APA, 1994, p. 594):

1. Recurrent episodes of binge eating. An episode of binge eating is characterized by both of the following:
    a. Eating, in a discrete period of time (e.g., within any two-hour period), an amount of food that is definitely larger than most people would eat during a similar period of time and under similar circumstances.
    b. Eating, in a discrete period of time (e.g., within any two-hour period), an amount of food that is definitely larger than most people would eat during a similar period of time and under similar circumstances. (2) A sense of lack of control

over eating during the episode (e.g., a feeling that one cannot stop eating or control what or how much one is eating).

2. Recurrent inappropriate compensatory behavior in order to prevent weight gain, such as self-induced vomiting; misuse of laxatives, diuretics, enemas, or other medications; fasting; or excessive exercise.

3. The binge eating and inappropriate compensatory behaviors both occur, on average, at least twice a week for three months.

4. Self-evaluation is unduly influenced by body shape and weight.

5. The disturbance does not occur exclusively during episodes of Anorexia Nervosa.

Diagnostic and Statistical Manual (DSM-IV): The fourth edition of the APA's medical classification system widely used in psychiatry and mental health settings. The DSM provides empirically based, clear definitions and criteria for all recognized mental disorders.

Disordered Eating: Atypical eating or disordered eating is far more common and widespread than clinical eating disorders. This term refers to troublesome eating behaviors that occur less frequently or are less severe than the behaviors required for the diagnosis of a clinical eating disorder. Disordered eating can be

changes in eating patterns that occur in relation to a stressful

event, an illness, personal appearance, or in preparation for

athletic competition. Many times, researchers that fail to

control for EDNOS, yield significant results of their sample that

fall below the criteria for anorexia and / or bulimia. Although

researchers may term this as disordered eating, it is assumed

they should be classified as EDNOS.

Eating Disorder: "Characterized by severe disturbances in eating

behavior" (APA, 2004, p. 583). Death rates from eating

disorders are the highest for any mental illness. There are three

clinical categories of eating disorders listed by the DSM-IV: 1)

Anorexia Nervosa, 2) Bulimia Nervosa, and 3) Eating Disorder–

Not Otherwise Specified.

Eating Disorder Bodybuilding Type (EDBT): Developed by Gruber

and Pope in 2000, this classification or grouping of criterions is

unrecognized by the APA and has not been included in any

studies beyond Gruber and Pope's 2000 research. Gruber and

Pope defines the criterion for EDBT as individuals having a rigid

adherence to a high-calorie, high-protein, low-fat diet that is

consumed in the form of pre-prepared meals and / or

supplements eaten at regularly scheduled intervals. People with

this disorder frequently refuse to eat out at restaurants or at

friends' houses because of their need to be certain that they

were ingesting the precise amounts of calories, protein, fat and

carbohydrates that they believed necessary to maintain their

physique. This proposed sub-clinical eating disorder category

may be included in the forthcoming DSM-V to be released in

2011 (Gruber & Pope, 2000).

Eating Disorder Bodybuilding Type (EDBT) Diagnostic Criteria
(Gruber & Pope, 2000):

1. Engage in regular episodes of binge eating without
   purging (examples of purging are: excessive exercise,
   self-induced vomiting, restriction of food, etc.)
2. Take steps to maintain a low level of body fat (below
   12%) accompanied by a desire to maximize muscle
   mass.

3. Intense fear of gaining fat or losing muscle, even though body fat is below normal, as defined above, and degree of muscularity is far above average.

4. Strict adherence to a rigid diet with at least two of the following features:

   a. At least five meals per day, consumed on a regular schedule, for example every three hours.

   b. Meals all consist of high-calorie, high-protein, low-fat foods or supplements.

   c. A significant amount of time and money is spent acquiring, preparing and eating these specialized meals.

5. Disturbance in the way in which one's body composition is experienced or undue influence of body appearance on self-evaluation.

6. Social and occupational opportunities are frequently given up because they interfere with the composition or timing of meals.

Eating Disorder Not Otherwise Specified (EDNOS): Individuals engaging in some form of abnormal eating but do not exhibit all the specific symptoms required for a diagnosis of anorexia nervosa or bulimia nervosa. According to the DSM-IV, "The presentation conforms to the general guidelines for a mental disorder in the diagnostic class, but the symptomatic picture does not the criteria for any of the specific disorders. This would occur either when the symptoms are below the diagnostic threshold for one of the specific disorders or when there is an atypical or mixed presentation" (APA, 2004, p. 4).

Varsity Sport Team: The principal team representing the institution in organized sport competitions, as it is distinctly different in culture and membership from a club or recreational team.

Significance of the Study

Decades of eating disorder studies have excluded males and even with its clinical standing, have also excluded the EDNOS category. This pattern has led to a clear literary void. As a result, myths and stereotypes were formed and augmented, becoming so ingrained into the American culture that they have been found to bias and hinder clinical judgments and medical diagnoses. Theoretically, advancement in this area will lead to a better understanding of eating disorders by contributing to eating disorder etiology and promoting a true presence of the disease. Furthermore, a more truthful account of ill males may reduce the disease's stigma through an increased social awareness that the disease's effects are equally severe to both genders. As a result, ill males may come forth and physicians may hold a higher tolerance of the disease's gender neutrality. If forthcoming studies continue to agree with the gender commonalities of predisposing traits, than the sociological stigmatic view of males with eating disorders may lose credibility.

Summary

Eating disorders are a significant American health issue worthy of empirical attention on both genders. As articulated in the second chapter, pathogenic and maladaptive eating and exercising behaviors occur in masses within collegiate athletics. Although some of these behaviors do not meet the DSM-IV's criteria for anorexia or bulimia, some will meet the criteria for EDNOS. These serious individual and social implications will befall in part on higher education.

CHAPTER II: REVIEW OF THE LITERATURE

"The ability to work toward a goal, sacrifice present satisfaction for future reward, is what makes you good at athletics and good at starving yourself" (Angela Guarda, Johns Hopkins).

Prevalence of Eating Disorders

During the reign of the Roman Empire, wealthy, prestigious men ate until their stomachs were bulged and bloated. Further binging was possible due to relief from self-induced purging in the vomitorium (a room in which ancient Romans are alleged to have vomited deliberately during feasts). Today, eating disorder symptomology ranks fourth among negative health behaviors of college students (Garman, Hayduck, Crider & Hodel, 2004). Consequently, eating disorders have quietly become an emerging facet of the American college and university culture, specifically among the student-athlete population.

In 1689, the son of a cleric gave a written medical account of a self-starved teenage boy. Two hundred years later, a London physician termed this mystifying condition of nervous atrophy as anorexia nervosa. Recently, the American medical community classified anorexia, bulimia, and EDNOS as clinical mental disorders. Prior to this medical classification in 1980, research findings established a standard prevalence rate of one eating disordered male for every ten ill females (Wolf, 1991). However, the increased research on males in the mid and late 1990s led to a closer estimate of one anorexia male for every four females and one bulimic male in every eight to ten bulimic females (American Journal of Psychiatry, 2001). In 1999, a study by Nelson, Hughes, Katz and Searlight produced an even closer ratio among genders. Challenging the ten to one ratio, the authors reported twenty and 10% of females and males respectively display eating disorder symptoms. Although the authors sought for indicators, not diagnoses, their finding was noteworthy because of the near equal degree of eating disorder symptoms males possess. This added credence to the "lower than reported" male prevalence rate that experts believe. Medical professionals and males often fail to notice eating disorder symptoms that are easily reported in females. Nelson,

Hughes, Katz and Searlight (1999) were able to produce a close ratio between genders by inquiring for symptoms that are traditionally ignored in men. Moreover, the majority of this study's college student sample was female (471), as only 333 were male. Even with this disproportional sample of genders, a two to one ratio was still found.

At present, it is suspected that the male prevalence rate for clinical eating disorders has increased from ten to 16% (Cohn, 2000). American health officials reported an increase of male eating disorder cases by 30% since 1972 stated Cohn, in her article *Fat is Not Just a Feminist Issue Anymore* (2000). Adding to this problem, both science and society perceive concerns over body fat as a women's issue.

This has led to men being undiagnosed and excluded from treatment for eating disorders. According to Cohn (2000), "In many ways, men are being discriminated against. People think something must be wrong with a man if he has an eating disorder." According to Richard Gordon's 2002 book, *Eating Disorders: Anatomy of a Social Epidemic*, he found an increase of male diagnoses. As a direct result, therapists are counseling

50% more males for eating disorders than compared to the mid-

1980s. Even with inherent difficulties of diagnosing the disease

among males, half of all Americans personally know someone

with an eating disorder.

The higher prevalence rates in the last decade have

elevated eating disorders to be a major American health

problem as the number of reported cases have increased to

"epidemic proportions" (Picard, 1999, p. 11). Five to ten million

Americans are diagnosed with eating disorders as are seventy

million people worldwide (Crowther, Wolf, & Sherwood, 1992).

Thirty-five percent of "normal dieters" progress to pathological

dieting. Of those, 20% to 25% advance to partial or full eating

disorders (Shisslak & Crago, 1995). An estimated 0.5% to 3.7%

of American females suffer from anorexia, while a bulimic

diagnosis is more common at 1.1% to 4.2%. Nationally, the

appearance of eating disorders in men is a growing

phenomenon. Yet a physician diagnosis and self-reporting of

this disease is severely lacking among males. Males represent one in six eating disorder sufferers, but only one in fifteen

patients seek treatment (Graham, 2004). Therefore, the

accepted male prevalence rate of 10% is conservative and not

inclusive of the undetected and undiagnosed. Of these reported

male cases, five to 8% are bulimic, with anorexia representing

one to 3%. Health officials report instances of male eating

disorders have increased 30% since 1972 (Graham, 2004). With

these figures, moderate estimates suggest one million American

males and ten million females are medically diagnosed with an

eating disorder.

Although EDNOS is not a "popular" eating disorder

category, its' significance and promise to eating disorder

etiology is the foundation of this essay. An EDNOS diagnosis

occurs when the 4th edition of the Diagnostic and Statistical

Manual of Mental Disorders (DSM-IV) criteria for anorexia or

bulimia is not met, yet a set degree of eating disorder

symptoms are present. Studies that have controlled for an

EDNOS diagnosis have found an approximate 20% to 65% of

their sample's eating disorders fall into this category (Black et al., 2003; Button, 2005; Carlat, Camargo, & Herzog, 1997; Ricca, Mannucci, and Mezzani, 2001; and Mitchell, 1986). Moreover, because the EDNOS criteria are not exclusionary to males, most eating disordered men fall within this category. Unfortunately, the EDNOS category and males remain severely under-researched. As a result, a literary void was formed - advancing social biases and medical complications that this review addresses.

Eating disorders are recognized as a psychiatric illness since they exceed normal concerns over body weight and image. Research conducted in the past fifteen years recognized college varsity athletes as having elevated rates of eating disorders, especially in selected sports. As discussed in the literature review, incidences of eating disorders in athletes are augmented when compared to the general population. In a 1999 study of 1,445 college athletes Johnson, Powers and Dick classified 58% of their sample as "high-risk" for developing an eating disorder (disordered eating). With this study, as in most, the researchers only controlled for anorexia and bulimia, excluding the third clinical eating disorder category of EDNOS. It is fair to assume that a significant portion of these "high-risk" athletes would meet the criteria of EDNOS.

Although athletes have a higher risk, many display eating disorder symptoms, but do not meet the diagnostic criteria for anorexia or bulimia. Because of the DSM-IV's narrow measures for anorexia and bulimia, the less rigid EDNOS standards have become the most convivial diagnosis for athletes and males. Thus, the EDNOS category has allowed the great divergence of males and females that display pathogenic eating behaviors to access treatment when they fall short of anorexia and bulimia criteria (DePalma, Koszewski, Romani, 2002; Sundgot-Borgen, 1994a, 1994b).

Still, conceptually speaking, the lack of research on the EDNOS category has left this category widely undiscovered even as EDNOS symptoms are severe and have the same threat as anorexia or bulimia to one's health and quality of life (Fries, 1977). Eating disorders have the highest premature fatality rate of all mental illnesses. Without treatment, 20% of those with an eating disorder will die. The government reports 50,000 deaths yearly from eating disorder complications. If treated, the mortality rate will drop 2% or 3%. With treatment, approximately 60% recover fully. This population maintains a healthy weight and consumes a variety of foods. They often form meaningful friendships, intimate relationships, and successful careers. Another 20% partially recover. This population often maintains peripheral relationships since their priority remains on food and exercise. The remaining 20% will not recover. They may have employment, but seldom have a meaningful career. The time spent on their fixation remains obligatory and their structure with food and exercise prohibits the investment in any other type of relationship. Furthermore, the majority of their disposable income is spent on low-calorie "safe" foods, fitness club membership, diet books, and the like.

In many reports, eating disorders are described as a continuum of disordered eating behaviors. This view of eating disorders is described by Rhodes' book *Life Inside the Thin Cage* and show in Figure 1. These are varying levels of disturbed food or exercise behaviors. According to Margaret Higham, Medical

Director of Tufts Health Services, eating disorders are a

"spectrum of behaviors - some people fall into strict categories

while some have milder symptoms, but they all deserve

attention" (Bergeron, 2004). This continuum of disordered

eating is helpful for clinicians to recognize eating concerns

among patients who do not fall into strict diagnostic categories,

hence, the value and importance of the EDNOS category.

Nature of Eating Disorders

*"The lure of starving - the baffling, seductive hook - was that it
soothed, a balm of safety and containment that seemed to
remove me from the ordinary, fraught world of human hunger
and place me high above it, in a private kingdom of calm"*
(Knapp, 2003, p. 7).

There are many facets that control eating behaviors:

appetite, food availability, cultural practices, family and peer

influences, and voluntary control. Eating disorders are serious

disturbances in eating behaviors. Researchers cited in this

review investigate the roots of abnormal voluntary control.

Eating disorders do not originate from a lack of resolve. They are of enormous complexity whereas specific maladaptive behaviors of eating and / or exercising are protected in a cycle of control and self-expression.

Eating disorders are complex in nature. The disease predominantly affects the mind by distorting thought processes. This dysfunctional psychology results in self-loathing and harm of the body. With irony, eating disorder cases generally occur in people of high intellect; yet the disease's control over one's thought process yields an impedance to accept even basic reasoning and logic to slightly normalize dysfunctional eating or exercising behaviors. This inability to change abnormal behaviors is rooted in the strong and desperate guard of the disorder, for at one time the illness served as a shield from a personal hardship. This unhealthy, yet effective coping method will manage a crisis by numbing natural emotions, providing a distraction from reality. Although facing a harsh, emotionally filled realism is avoided, this suppression prohibited a healthy process of grieving. By not managing the hardship, the unfelt numbed emotions were suppressed, only to be replaced by

eating disorder behaviors that remain until the natural grieving

process no longer delayed.

Although a paralyzing disease, eating disorders evolve

into a lifestyle, drawing striking parallels to religion. With

fundamental likenesses, it is clear why historically eating

disorders became intertwined with the Catholic faith. Both

eating disorder and religion are relied upon during times of

distress. A personal relationship is formed rooted in faith, not

fact or reason. Both provide structure in rules for "righteous"

daily living and guides one's way of life. Personal sacrifice and

meekness are often at the center of both. These values, or

convictions taken to an extreme, are often revered by others.

The religion of an eating disorder is very personal - providing

comfort, trust, pride, structure, sacrifice, rules, and the ability to

manage crisis. Outside interventions to dismiss these beliefs /

rules can be perceived as an attack on one's personal beliefs as

the intervention is essentially requesting one to renounce their

religion. A fear to release an eating disorder can be rooted in losing a part of one's identity and esteem, as the eating disorder

manufactures an artificial facade of individuality, strength, and

pride. In essence, to recover is to abandon deep convictions and

become vulnerable.

With this clarification that is deeper than the popular

notions, three hundred years of research confirmed eating

disorders refocus emotional pain on the ill self-treatment of the

body. Consequently, the medical classification of 1980 was a

reversal of early beliefs that the disease was a nervous

condition of choice. Medical research established that

disordered eating originates in the unconscious, allowing

victims to cope with and survive traumas by yielding a strict

control of food intake and exercise routines. Yet this truth is not

shared by popular culture. The societal view of eating disorders

remains as a chosen illness, a preferred means to thinness by

wealthy, white females.

When predisposed people lose their sense of control

because of an event that is forced upon them, their balance of

control is altered. One's power over eating and exercising aids in regaining this loss of control by increasing the mastery over self through personal sacrifice and pain. This expression of control is a protection, defense, and distraction; for the compulsion of one's food choices and amounts, or degree of exercise cannot be "taken away" or "changed" by another. An eating disordered person is fixated on controlling specific behaviors since these aspects may feel like the only part of their life that cannot "leave" unless it is one's own decision. Symbolically, this overcompensates for the loss felt in the violation that triggered the disease's onset. The dependability of this comfort only deepens one's reliance on their behaviors and validates their resolution (Andersen, 2001; Kaye, Klump, Frank, & Strober, 2000; Rogers & Petrie, 2001; & Vitousek et al., 1998).

Cultural pressures placed upon both genders to achieve unrealistic body shapes partly explain the eating disorder's root. However, a combination of multiple factors influences the disease's onset. This is especially true for "cultures that place a very high premium on appearance and highly value thinness and portray that in their media" (Bergeron, 2004). Commonly

known agitators of the disease are low self-esteem, perceived

lack of life control, depression, anxiety, troubled personal

relationships, difficulty expressing emotions or feelings, and

history of physical or sexual abuse. According to Higham,

Medical Director of Tufts Health Services, "The disorder is there

for a reason - the behavior serves a positive purpose in their life

and someone suffering from an eating disorder can't get better

until the disadvantages of the behavior outweigh the

advantages" (Bergeron, 2004).

As shown in Figure 6 created by Nathenshon for his

1999 book, *When Your Child has an Eating Disorder*, there is not

a single root of an eating disorder. Biological, social, and

psychological aspects intersect and share aspects in the

disease's onset and progression. Most eating disorders originate

in predisposed persons that had an experience that threatened

their sense of control. A common change that is proven to

elevate the risk of an eating disorder is the transition to college

from high school. This or another perceived threat could cause unconscious fixations that over-adjust for the loss of control. As

eating disorders lie in the realm of one's psyche, it is difficult for

those without the knowledge or experience of the disease to

fully understand its depth and profound influence on one's way

of life.

The common approach by loved ones to encourage a

behavioral change in disturbed eating and exercising patterns is

often futile as the disease's manipulation and dominance over

food and exercise is often not susceptible to reason or logic. The

disease's depth of illogical perceptions of reality can be

mentally exhausting to understand for both the eating

disordered person and their loved ones. Rather, the individual

must resolve the underlying issue(s) that caused the need for

the disease. In addition, because an eating disorder is ones

foremost coping skill, a component of recovery is relearning and

trusting healthy ways to manage stress, conflict, and change.

While this is a difficult process, healthy coping strategies may

allow one to overcome adversity without resorting to the

instant comfort provided by unhealthy eating and / or

exercising behaviors. Consequently, these new coping skills must be fully trusted before the protection from the eating disorders is abandoned.

Understandably, it is difficult for those with normal eating behaviors to understand the depth of this overpowering, consuming, selfish, and burdensome disease. The protection of the disease from the emotions brought about by change or abandonment is motivated by the disease's role as protector – providing the ability to cope with adversity and creating a sense of identity and esteem (Dolhanty, 1998). The eating disorder and its behaviors can be the sole form of personal pride and achievement by adhering to strict rules that are perceived as unattainable by others because of the high level of personal commitment needed to sustain the behaviors. Without the self-control provided by the disease's rules, there is an intense fear of reality if the safeties of these rules are abandoned (Dolhanty, 1998). Ending these deeply personal behaviors is regard as a betrayal that will cause emotional vulnerability and unwanted physical changes. One's eating disorder rules are protected and revered since they manage by repressing a significant hardship

or event. Often, people with eating disorders refer to their

disease as their "best friend," for without it, they fear a life of

loneliness and weakness without control or recourse.

To best describe the immense power of the disease's

control, in her book, *Appetites: Why Women Want* (2003),

Caroline Knapp's lure of self-starvation was encapsulated in the

purest sense, as her anorexic behaviors made her feel

"supremely safe: one concern, one feeling, everything else just

background noise [emphasis mine] (p. 7)". Knapp's quote

provides an insight that simply and accurately defines the allure

offered by an eating disorder - the focus on one aspect; ignoring

and repressing painful experiences. The disease is a detachment

from reality, the reduction of every aspect of one's self to

"background noise." With the insight Knapp offers, it is common

for the cycle of obsession to cause considerable inattention to

personal and professional obligations and poor life choices.

Consequently, the deterioration of relationships and careers are

common, often resulting in an isolated and poor quality of life.

If eating disorders are more than just meticulous eating habits, than food rituals and exercise routines are only symptoms, that is, a visible byproduct of the disease. Controlled eating and exercising are skillful techniques that manage and conceal a host of feelings often hidden or ignored for years. Most people with an eating disorder tend to be of a high intelligence, but have a painfully intense sense of inadequacy, unworthiness, and inferiority (Scott, 1988). Thus, people with eating disorders often fall into a reclusive state. In 1999, Nelson, Hughes, Katz and Searlight's study reported that people with eating disorders were "remarkable for their academic achievement (p. 630)." Control over food and body creates a temporary feeling of euphoria, a relief of buried emotions. One often feels very powerful with a strong sense of pride in their eating disorder and the ability to suppress temptations in which "weak" people indulge. This endless fixation with power and control over self-deprivation allows one to ignore, subdue, and manage their past trauma(s) that is now rooted in a compulsion to feel euphoric in their superiority over others by their elite self-control, discipline, and adherence to a strict, limited, and pleasureless routine.

Without this preoccupation of control, an eating disordered person believes they are ill equipped to cope with adversity, failure, and their residing guilt. Trust in their disease may serve as their only source of dependability – as it is absent of the fears of change or abandonment. Ironically, but not by coincidence, the initial trauma often had aspects of change or abandonment. As the disease helped one through distressing times of suffering, the eating disorder metaphorically became one's best friend. This personal relationship helps to keep the commitment to preserve and protect the relationship with the disease. This dependency is strengthened by one's indebtedness that is rooted in the disease numbing the effect of a crisis. The fear of losing the ability to again become completely numb is compounded by the unconscious fear of addressing the past hardship. This is the most complex aspect for the ill person to overcome and for loved ones to understand.

Restrictive (anorexic) or binge (bulimic) eating are flawed relationships with food, but food or the abuse of exercise is not a complete representation of the disease. The most wounding component of an eating disorder is the permeation and control on the psyche through ruminating thoughts. Normalized eating does not signify recovery. One can robotically consume a meal considered "normal," yet still mask feelings of inadequacy, worthlessness, and guilt. Regaining personal trust and control over one's self is recovery. Unfortunately, these signs of healing are the most difficult to recapture and rebuild, as one must release the deep trust in their eating disorder while ignoring temptations rooted in fear.

As eating disorders are deeper than mere weight shifts and food and exercise obsessions, the deterioration of the body is a symptom from a misdirected and flawed attempt to manage a crisis. Often and unfortunately, the media promotes fallacies that contribute to stereotypical views. This study directly challenges many of these myths by conducting valid scholarly research on understudied facets of eating disorders. This is achieved by controlling for three often excluded, but relevant

variables in eating disorder scholarship: 1) An exclusive male

sample; 2) Measuring the presence of the EDNOS and the sub-

clinical disordered eating and EDBT categories; and 3) Surveying

an array of male inhabited sports. Assumedly, by controlling for

these often-excluded variables, the study's findings will

contradict the fabric these popular misconceptions. It is with

irony that the review of the literature explores the etiology of

eating disorder research dating back to the second century that

began with a male subject, not a female, as the first recorded

eating disorder case.

Reasons for Male Underestimation

*"Anorexia may be under-diagnosed because many physicians, as
well as the anorexics themselves, are unaware that this
condition occurs in both sexes"* (Strumia, Manzato, & Gualandi,
2002, p. 464).

One interested in researching eating disorders will

quickly learn that a physician diagnosis and self-identification or

reporting is difficult with males. People with eating disorders often do not recognize or admit their illness. Because of the secretiveness and shame associated with eating disorders, many cases are not reported. As a medical intervention is postponed or absent, eating disorders prevalence rates are greatly underestimated. Yet modest statistics reveal almost seventy-million people worldwide suffer from a disease that affects one's mental and physical well-being. With 80% of American women reporting body shape dissatisfaction and a host of reasons for a male misdiagnosis, medical diagnosis and treatment is frequently delayed or absent (Smolak, 1996). Paul Mueller, spokesperson for Rogers Memorial Hospital - the nation's first residential eating disorder program for men - states male eating disorders always existed: "There was always a persistence of anorexia and bulimia [among men]. It's just now being more widely recognized." (McCormak, 2000)

In past decade, it is presumed the number of men with eating disorder symptoms has doubled (Natenshon, 1999). New research from the University of Toronto established that one of every six people with full or partial anorexia is male (Natenshon,

1999). This estimate is substantially greater than the customary representation of one in ten. This largely under-recognized / reported population is most likely to associate unnatural weight loss to a physical issue, rather than a psychological concern. Additionally, males are forbidden in the American society to be concerned about their appearance, therefore the increased motivation to keep their body image obsessions private.

Contrary to popular opinion, people with eating disorders may fall within healthy weight ranges or even be overweight. The danger of the disease lies within eating disorder patterns of behaviors. Without a true relation of body weight to disease, many symptoms are unnoticed. Common food indicators are often overlooked such as restriction of specific foods, eating in solitary, cutting food into small pieces, habitually eating "safe foods", conducting "food rituals", preparing meals for others, consumption of an abnormal amount of water or caffeinated beverages, or a rotation of days of restricting and followed by normal eating. Many physician diagnoses are omitted because the medical community's unfamiliarity of the disease and the depth of the intertwined myths that are woven into the fabric of American culture.

Physicians often overlook an eating disorder among male patients from the lack of expectancy and less obvious symptoms. Supporting this claim, Strumia Manzato and Gualandi declared, "Anorexia may be under-diagnosed because many physicians, as well as the anorexics themselves, are unaware that this condition occurs in both sexes" (2002, p. 464). Subsequently, a diagnosis in a male will take more than three times as long when compared to a female. With this, the mean age of a male anorexia diagnosis is twenty-four as compared to the estimated ages of 14-18 for a female (APA, 2004). According to Crisp and Burns 1983 study, the male's age of diagnosis is about three to four years after the disease's onset.

Physicians rely on clear indicators in female patients, for example: menstrual cycle loss (amenorrhea) and the classic "female triad" (disordered eating, amenorrhea, and osteoporosis). Without these obvious and common signs, physicians must have the knowledge and insight to detect eating disorders in males. Yet with male patients, physicians often conclude an eating disorder diagnosis only after a dramatic shift in body weight. However, this simplistic means of diagnosis is flawed, as a low body weight is only one symptom, exclusive to anorexia – the category that includes the least amount of males. As opposed to females, this criterion is often deceptive in males with normal body weights due to the average or high degree of muscle mass. For men with an eating disorder, the primary physical symptoms are decreases in testosterone levels and sexual libido – signs likely to go unnoticed, unreported, or untested (Rader Programs, 2006). Furthermore, male bulimics often have a higher threshold in identifying a binge episode, as they are less likely to admit concerns of body weight and shape. Additionally, overeating (binging) is a more expectable societal norm in males. Yet the most prevailing aspect that prohibits a male diagnosis is the lower degree of suspicion that many physicians hold.

This diverging complexity among genders will often causes a late or absent male diagnosis. A delay in detection will position the ill person to develop a stronger connection to their eating. Consequently, the most serious outcome of a postponed diagnosis is the disease's progression and worsening of symptoms. With an average male diagnosis occurring between two and eleven years later than females, males are most likely to be detected in an advanced stage (Blinder, 2002; Anorexia Nervosa and Bulimia Association, 1997). Consequently, the physical and social ramifications of the disease are exacerbated, as is the ease of recovery. Because recovery is linked to the time of detection, and detection occurs later in males, the disease's longevity in males often results in chronic or debilitating results. Because of this low male detection rate, men can recover from eating disorders, but it is often a longer and more complex process. Relapse among males is more common and the impulse to engage in abnormal eating and compulsive exercise is often a lifelong struggle.

With the medical community's unfamiliarity with the less obvious male eating disorder symptomology, a diagnosis among men is often delayed or absent. Even with these complications, males are still diagnosed at a ratio of one to every ten females with an eating disorder. The significance of this aspect of eating disorders is the unknown extent of a true male prevalence rate.

Deconstructing the Male Myth

"Males with eating disorders have been relatively ignored, neglected, dismissed because of statistical infrequency or legislated out of existence by theoretical dogma" (Arnold Anderson, 1990, p. 119).

Routinely viewed as a self-imposed condition for middle and upper-middle class girls and women, research has determined this disease is among all racial, social, and economic levels (Person, Benson-Quaziena, & Rogers, 2001; Anderson & Mickalide, 1983.). Yet this stigma remains in Western popular culture. Adding to the misconception, researchers regularly sample adolescent and young adult females that are predominantly white and from middle and upper class backgrounds. This contributes to the misrepresentation of prevalence rates across differing populations. As such, common beliefs, publications, and educational programs are not truly indicative of the American populace because of their selectivity of gender, race, socio-economic status, and their limitation to the categories of anorexia and bulimia.

Clearly, eating disorders are not limited to females, nor do the effects of the disease only result from the categories of anorexia and bulimia. Males suffer from all three types of eating disorders - the third category, EDNOS, being the most prevalent, understudied, and misunderstood. The strict DSM-IV criteria for anorexia and bulimia cause most eating disordered males to be classified under the EDNOS category. Aside from the EDNOS category, disordered eating and the pending EDBT category has the prospective to epitomizing many ill males. Despite this clear void, only a handful researchers design their studies to include the EDNOS category. Furthermore, a male sample without controlling for athletic participation in studies is rare. Within these studies, select groups of sports with an established high prevalence rate are frequently used. This method excludes other sports that may test high for EDNOS presence rates. Researchers whom consider the EDNOS category among males often yield significantly high prevalence rates and implore their peers to direct future research on these two understudied areas with a promise of significance to the field of eating disorders.

Because of the disproportional occurrences of eating disorders among genders, the majority of authors continually center their research on female samples. As a result, the myth and stigma of eating disorders as a female disease is preserved. Consequentially, this misperception breeds ignorance, uncertainty, and embarrassment for a myriad of males suffering from the disease. These males often remain without support and treatment. As a result, males are diagnosed at a much later age; recover over a longer period of time, and relapses more often. Yet research, literature, and the social familiarity of females with anorexic and bulimia are abounding and extensive in content. Arnold Anderson, a leading researcher and expert on eating disorders states in his 1990 book, *Males with Eating Disorders*, for the necessity to improve male detection rates through research that will widen the narrow focus of literature by "presenting intellectual challenges regarding the etiology and mechanism for this gender-divergent abnormality of human-motivated behavior" (Anderson, 199, p. 223).

Divergence of Gender Symptomology

The preponderance of studies agrees that eating disorder symptomology does not differ greatly among sexes. Nearly all of the underlying traits identified to predispose and contribute to the onset of eating disorders are the same for both genders. These predisposing traits include perfectionism, over-achieving, anxiety, depression, low self-esteem, self-loathing, avoidance of conflict, perceived loss of control, identity conflicts, inability to cope with or express emotions, need for acceptance, and an unhealthy family communication structure (Johnson, 1994). American health officials estimate 22.1% of its citizenry above the age of 18, or one in five adults, are diagnosed with a mental illness. Using statistics from the

1988 census, this translates to 44.3-million residential

Americans diagnosed with a mental illness. In America, 50% of

those diagnosed with an eating disorder also met the criteria for

depression (Renfrew Center Foundation).

American culture values athleticism. In turn, there is a

strong masculine ideal for boys and men. Eating disordered men

report having difficulty fitting into the masculine values of

competitiveness, aggressiveness, strength, athleticism, and

independence. Boys who later develop eating disorders tend to

be more passive and dependent than their normalized eating

male counterparts. Within the American society, men do not

have the social "permission" to verbally express their feelings

and emotions. Since childhood, males are taught and groomed

to be "in control," "tough it out," and handle problems

themselves. As situations occur that prohibit a male to retain his

control, he may perceive this inability as a personal weakness or

a failure. Consequently, predisposed persons will over-adjust for

this perceived lack of control by substituting an undue amount of control over food and / or exercise (Piracy, 1999). Within this realm of pathogenic behaviors, a person will appear disciplined and powerful by suppressing pleasure and displaying an unrivaled devotion and strength to their convictions. These socially admired characteristics (discipline and devotion) only serve to mask the disease. With gender-biased stigmas in place, an ill male can be overlooked while the same symptoms would cause alarm in a female. Consequently, the stigma of eating disorders often makes males reluctant to seek treatment.

Other slight variations of the disease have been reported to manifest differently among men. In these selected studies, minor discrepancies among genders were found. One study noticed male anorexics were more physically active by using excessive exercise as their foremost method of purging and had fewer episodes of binging, vomiting, and laxative abuse. In this study, males were more achievement oriented and preoccupied with their food choices (Schneider & Argas, 1987). These achievement and perfectionism traits may add to the disease's presence among male athletes in their pursuit of individual excellence.

Another study established a difference among genders in processing events. A negative life experience to a male often remains internalized, leading him to be disconnected and ashamed of his body. Research has proved that men with eating disorders tend to be more concerned with body size and shape, whereas women are more preoccupied with body weight (Cororve & Gleaves, 2001). Central to their eating disorder, men are prone to exercise excessively as their preferred method of purging. Women mostly purge through self-induced vomiting and laxatives. Bulimia among males is far more common than anorexia, as an estimated one to 3% of female and one out of ten males develop this eating disorder. Even though both genders experience bulimia at nearly the same rates, men tend to react with less self-hatred and less occurrences of self-induced vomiting. Thus, female self-induced vomiting is four to five times more prevalent than among males.

Kearny-Cooke and Steichen-Asch's 1990 study, *Men,*

Body Image, and Eating Disorders found that males with eating

disorders tended to be dependent, avoidant, and passive-

aggressive. The study's results also indicated males were prone

to body image distortions - believing themselves to be fat when,

in fact, they were very thin; or with EDBT, believing themselves

to be thin as they are muscular. In a murky array of certain

forewarning, body image concerns are a strong indicator of

eating disorders in males. As previously stated, low sex drive,

decreased testosterone, and sexual anxiety are exclusive to

eating disordered males, yet are likely to be unnoticed,

unreported, and untested.

Arnold Anderson upheld the similarities of eating

disorders among genders proven in his empirical studies and

clinical trials. However, Anderson believes that as the symptoms

are "deconstructed" through psychological treatment, gender

differences are clearly revealed within one's predisposition,

course of the disease's development, and onset. Anderson

states, "We have to go back to where the roots are formed and look at gender diversity" (Knowlton, 1995, p. 1). From his more than thirty-years in the field, Anderson cites patterns of females feeling overweight, as men are truly overweight prior to developing an eating disorder. This indicator for males often remains unnoticed because of Western culture's bias of accepting overweight and overeating males. Anderson also believes males tend to be unduly concerned with body shape and muscle definition. In his treatment of males, Anderson has observed a male tendency to restrict and adhere to consuming specific foods for athletic achievements (Knowlton, 1995). Lastly, Anderson acknowledges males with eating disorders tend to display obsessive features and are commonly misdiagnosed with ADD, ADHD, or OCD.

In 1997, Carlat, Camargo, and Herzog completed a study fittingly entitled *Eating Disorders in Males*. As the research team sampled 135 eating disordered males in a hospital setting, they found a majority also suffered from depressive disorders (80%). A noteworthy feature of the study was the unexpected high prevalence of the EDNOS category: 46% bulimic; 32% EDNOS;

and 22% anorexic. From their study, Carlat, Camargo, and Herzog concluded males and females with eating disorders have shared attributes with the exception of an increased likelihood of bulimia in homosexual and bisexual males.

A secondary finding from Nelson, Hughes, Katz, and Searight's 1999 research was their sample's unwarranted fears of increasing body fat and being overweight even as their caloric intake fell below their needed daily expenditures. Sixty-six percent of their male sample was "terrified" about being overweight; 61% obsessed about burning calories during exercise; and 59% revealed they have ruminating thoughts about the fat on their bodies. As these psychological disturbances are shared among genders, the study revealed higher occurrences of psychological distress among eating disordered males. Adding to these concerns, the male sample also reported difficulty conforming to traditional American societal roles – a similar result found in Piracy's 1999 research. Stemming from his inability to fit into traditional male societal role, the sample had difficultly identifying with their fathers.

Conversely, the researchers found their sample had closer mother-son relationships, and distant father-son connections.

Further studies support gender neutrality and family dynamics in the development of eating disorders. Fitcher and Daser (1987) allege that male anorexics perceived themselves as more feminine then other men in their attitudes and behaviors. Mothers often relate more with their daughters emotionally than physically. Fathers typically take a contradictory approach, communicating to their sons through physical play. If a son is not proficient at sports, he may feel he has disappointed his father and is responsible for losing their sole means of communication. As did Nelson, Hughes, Katz, and Searight in their 1999 study, Fitcher and Daser (1987) also found eating disordered men commonly identify more closely with their mother than fathers.

Origin of Eating Disorder Research

"Do not allow the body to attain extreme thinness for that too is treacherous, but bring it only to a condition which will naturally continue unchanged, whatever that may be" (Hippocrates, 400 B.C.).

In the Hellenistic era, Sir William Gull was the first known author to comment and document the act of self-starvation. Gull referred to this form of self-abuse interchangeably, using the terms "hysteria" and "anorexia nervosa" (Pearce, 2004). Gull's essays reflected his observations of 11th century stanch Catholic females severely restricting their food intake as an act of self-sacrifice for their religious convictions. These religious ascetics renounced material comforts of the "evil corporeal world" to lead a life of austere and self-discipline (Pearce, 2004, p. 191). These "holy anorexics," as Gull referred, or "fasting saints" as they are now known, sought religious refuge, rejected marriage, and often died from their personal sacrifice of starvation. As the Roman Empire ended, the occurrence of "holy anorexics" declined until the 19th century. In the Dark Ages, historians acknowledge only a few known cases, mostly of young women thought to be possessed by Satan and cured by exorcism of starvation.

In 383 AD, St. Jerome fled to Bethlehem after a female follower died from self-starvation. Historians agree this is the first recorded anorexic death (Pearce, 2004). The strong convictions of these "holy anorexics" to restrict bodily pleasures until death were a factor in their rise to sainthood (Pearce, 2004). Many saints, such as Saint Catherine of Siena (1347-1380), starved themselves as a "route to God" (Pearce, 2004, p. 192). Saint Theresa of Avila also starved herself, used twigs of olives to induce vomiting, and only allowed the Host (sacrament of communion) as her only source of food sustenance. In her eighteenth year of age (1684), St. Mary Axe's severe anorexic behaviors suppressed her menstrual cycle as her physician observed that "cares and passions of her mind" did not address her failing health. In excerpts from the notes of St. Mary's physician, he also stated:

I do not remember that I did ever in all my practice see one that was conversant with the living so much wasted with the greatest degree of consumption like a skeleton only clad with skin. A nervous atrophy, or consumption, is a wasting of the body without any remarkable fever, cough, or shortness of breath; but it is attended with a want of appetite, and a bad digestion, upon which there follows a languishing weakness of nature, and a falling away of the flesh every day more and more"

(Pearce, 2004, p. 192).

In his article on the history of anorexia, Pearce (2004) discussed Robert Whytt of Edinburgh, Scotland. In 1764, Whytt identified the associated bradycardia (slow heart rate) of anorexics and described the bodily wasting of anorexics as a "nervous atrophy" (Pearce 2004, p. 192). In the 19th century, Sigmund Freud recorded the first case of bulimia in a female patient. The first written account of an anorexic patient was by Louis-Victor

Marce in 1859 (1828-1864). In 1873, two neurologists - Ernest

Charles Lasègue and Claude Bernard separately depicted

symptoms of anorexia nervosa.

Lasègue, a French internist, born and died in Paris

(1816-1883) and obtained his doctorate in Paris in 1847. In

1862, Lasègue lectured on diseases of the brain and nerves,

becoming professor of clinical medicine at the Hôpital Necker in

1869 and held this tenure until his death. He wrote that the

refusal of food "may be indefinitely prolonged" (Pearce 2004, p.

191). From Lasègue's medical journals, Pearce (2004) was able

to decipher Lasègue's early attempts of understanding anorexic

behaviors.

> Go back in the history of the patient, and if you
>
> search you will find the 'ictus' which suddenly
>
> destroyed his mental balance. From then on,
>
> the brain is like a piano from which certain keys
>
> have been removed and which, therefore,
>
> produces only imperfect and dissonant chords.

A refusal of food that may be indefinitely prolonged. Woe to the physician who, misunderstanding the peril, treats as a fancy without object or duration an obstinacy which he hopes to vanquish by medicines, friendly advice, or by the still more defective resource, intimidation. When after several months the family, the doctor, and the friends perceive the persistent inutility of all these attempts. The patient replies that it furnishes sufficient nourishment for her, adding that she is neither changed nor thinner. She says that she never was better. I might almost say a condition of contentment truly pathological. Not only does she not sigh for recovery, but she is not ill-pleased with her condition.

A particular form of disease characterized by extreme emaciation, and often referred to [as] latent tubercule, and mesenteric disease. The subjects of this affection are mostly of the female sex, and chiefly between the ages of 16 and 23. I have occasionally seen it in males at the same age. The patient complained of no pain, but was restless and active. This was in fact a striking expression of the nervous state, for it seemed hardly possible that a body so wasted could undergo the exercise which seemed agreeable. It will be observed that all the conditions in this case were negative, and may be explained by the anorexia which led to starvation, and a depression of all the vital functions; viz., amenorrhea, slow pulse, slow breathing (Lasègue's Medical Journals in Pearce 2004).

Historic cases of male starvation occurred in the 17th

and 18th centuries. Despite the before mentioned articulations

of symptomology, Richard Morton is credited with the first

medical description and documentation of anorexia nervosa in

1689. Morton (1637-1698), a son of a cleric, was born in Suffolk

and educated at Magdalen Hall, Oxford. After graduating in

1656, Morton became chaplain of New College. In 1670, he

abandoned his religious obligations and studied medicine at

Oxford. Morton was admitted to the College of Physicians in

1675, becoming a Fellow in 1678 and a Censor in 1690.

Morton's work on early anorexia is widely renowned, as he is

published in Phthisiologia and two other prestigious texts in

1692. Morton described his work with a sixteen-year-old eating

disordered male as a case of "nervous consumption"; a remedy

of horseback riding and absence from studies was prescribed by

Morton (Carlat, Camargo, & Herzog, 1997).

Philosophical debates emerged in the twentieth century

as researchers became divided on eating disorder philosophy.

Some believed eating disorders were a "purely psychological

malady" (Pearce 2004, p. 192), as others, such as Simmonds in 1914, proposed that "pituitary insufficiency led to weight loss" (Pearce 2004, p. 192). Jean-Martin Charcot studied the "intimate and reciprocal" relationship between the disciplines of psychiatry and photography in the late nineteenth century. Focusing on the patients with hysteria in the Salpetriere hospital, the notorious Parisian asylum for insane and incurable women, Charcot photographed and provided his skeptical colleagues with visual proof of hysteria's form. These images which appear in Charcot's album, *Iconographie Photographique de la Salpetriere* expanded on Sir William Gull's use of the term "anorexia hysterica" while advocating isolation as a life-saving initial treatment.

In his 1930 essays, Berkman acknowledged that deficiencies of pituitary hormones were secondary to the act of self-starvation, correctly believing that self-starvation was the cause of bodily ills. Another development in the early understanding of eating disorders was Bruch's 1979 book, *Golden Cage: The Enigma of Anorexia Nervosa* that established the association between eating disorders and the fear of obesity and body image distortion. Within this historic study, Bruch's findings advanced eating disorders from an emotional, nervous condition to a credible illness placed in medical footing. This discovery set the foundation for the clinical adoption of eating disorders as a mental illness in 1980. Burch's research spawned a generation of studies on the interaction of various conscious and unconscious mental and emotional processes, particularly as they influence personality, behavior, and attitudes.

Studies conducted in the 1980's became fundamentally significant to eating disorder etiology because the findings of these early studies allowed researchers to center on patterns of demographics, clinical features, disorder psychology, and treatment procedures. However, three-hundred years of research starting with an anorexic boy contains only a modest portion studying males or the category in which they most often fall. It is to this area of eating disorder scholarship we now turn.

Research on EDNOS

"The DSM-IV criteria are both a blessing and a curse. A blessing because this is better for research, but also a curse because clinically a lot of people who have really severe eating disorders don't meet the [anorexia or bulimia] DSM-IV criteria" (Eating Disorder Review, 1999).

More than three-hundred years following the discovery of anorexia by Dr. Richard Morton in an adolescent male, there has been a disproportionate amount of research on females with either anorexia or bulimia. The consequence of this bias has caused a substantial deficiency of knowledge on eating disordered males and the EDNOS category. Most often, studies with an exclusive male sample will only focus on athletic participation. Within these types of studies, the research is further restricted by only controlling for sports known to have high prevalence rates. Further limiting this already narrow scope of scholarship is the recurrent testing of anorexia and bulimia for most study's variables. It is a puzzling state as the "not otherwise specified" category is seldom measured even as studies with EDNOS as a variable produce statistically significant results of increased eating disorder prevalence, most notably

within the male population. In conversation with Ron

Thompson, a leading expert in the field of eating disorders, he

stated, "some believe (as do I) that it [EDNOS] is probably the

most prevalent diagnosis" (Ron Thompson, personal

communication, May 8, 2006). Even with limited studies on

males and EDNOS eating disorders, the field of research has

matured since its inception. In the following section, articles and

studies that include the EDNOS category are discussed to

further justify its inclusion in eating disorder research.

In the journal article, *Don't Forget EDNOS: Patterns of*

Service Use in an Eating Disorder Service, Button (2005)

physician referrals to an eating disorder clinic were tracked.

Ninety-six percent of the clinic's cliental were female and

patients had a median stay of 5.7 months. In a three year time

period, the EDNOS category prevailed as the most common

classification of the residents with a percentage of 43.8 (bulimia

accounted for 36.7% of patient diagnoses, 13.7% were classified

as having disordered eating, and 6.8% were anorexic). With

these figures, Button reported only one in nine patients were considered to have a clinical eating disorder. Thirty-six percent of the EDNOS patients partook in strenuous exercise as their preferred form of purging, while 32% used self-induced vomiting and 13% abused laxatives.

These results were similar to an earlier study by Ricca, Mannucci and Mezzani (2001) who reported a comparable number of EDNOS diagnoses of 43.8% among two eating disorder clinics. To best articulate the prevalence of the EDNOS diagnoses, over the three-year period of the study, only one out of every nine patients had bulimia or anorexia – the rest were EDNOS. Furthermore, the researchers found that approximately half of the clinic's outpatient was EDNOS diagnosed. In a direct sample of the clinic's EDNOS patients, Button found 36% abused exercise as their preferred form of purging. It has been suggested that exercise dependency is an underlying factor of eating disorders, an aspect that occurs frequently in studies on EDNOS. Other common forms of purging in EDNOS patients were self-induced vomiting (32%) and laxative abuse (13%).

Button also found EDNOS patients to hold similar attitudinal concerns of anorexics and bulimics, as 81% of EDNOS patients had an intense fear of gaining weight, 78% were distressed over their body image and shape, and 48% had a distorted body image. Ricca, Mannucci and Mezzani (2001) also found EDNOS patients held similar qualities of bulimics and anorexics, such as high levels of restrained eating, intense fears of gain weight, and distorted body images.

Button established that almost half of an eating disorder clinic's resources were utilized by the EDNOS population. Consequently, Button advised these mental health facilities to become better equipped to identify and treat this forthcoming population. Addressing the issue of EDNOS strains on clinic resources, Button stated,

> EDNOS patients are likely to form a major part of the [clinic's] demand. Such people should not be seen as presenting trivial symptoms and their need for help is similar to those with anorexia and bulimia. The substantial needs of

patients with EDNOS should be taken into

account in planning specialized services for

adults with eating disorders (Button, 2005, p.

134).

Researchers have estimated that three to 19% of college

women are bulimic; while one to 2% are anorexic (Powers,

Schulman, Gleghorn, & Prange, 1987; Mintz & Bentz, 1986). The

college environment tends to produce higher occurrences of

disordered eating behaviors in students as seen in Mintz and

Bentz's 1986 study that reported a 61% prevalence rate.

Although Mintz and Bentz failed to test for an EDNOS diagnosis,

they admitted the likelihood of the sample's 61% displaying

maladaptive and pathogenic behaviors might meet the EDNOS

criteria. With this, two points of consideration need to be

addressed. First, only females were included in the study. If

males were included, the already high rate of disordered eating

would likely increase, as males are most likely to have EDNOS

symptoms. Secondly, the female sample was not of student-

athletes. Athletic participation, particularly at a competitive level, is proven to yield elevated occurrences of eating

disorders.

Studies that consider the EDNOS classification among a

college population have produced high prevalence rates of

statistical significance. This spike of eating disorders within a

college population is derived from the comparable ages of the

traditional American college student and the disease's onset

and length. Another factor is the social pressures attached to

the transition from high school to college, an aspect discussed

in the later section on higher education. In 1987, Schotte and

Stinkard found almost half of their college student sample

displayed some form of abnormal eating behaviors. This finding

is consistent with other studies that have also sampled college

students. The most notable study is Engel et al. 2003 research

conducted in collaboration with the NCAA.

In the largest study to date on the eating attitudes and

behaviors of collegiate student-athletes, Engel and his team of

six researchers authored a 2003 study with the NCAA, entitled

Predictors of Disordered Eating in a Sample of Elite Division I

College Athletes. The study investigated the lifestyles of competitive athletes and measured for disordered eating behaviors. The study was designed to survey 1,445 Division I athletes at eleven separate institutions in eleven different sports. By using a hierarchical regression, all known predictors of the college experience that may be associated with disordered eating attitudes and symptomology was measured.

The study determined that certain predictors exist that suggest disordered eating student-athletes – such as demographics, athletic involvement, and personality. The study established a prediction between 40.5 and 46.4% of the sample fell into a disordered eating category by restricted food, and scoring high on body dissatisfaction and drive for thinness surveys. Of the eleven sports considered, wrestling and gymnastics exhibited the highest levels of drive for thinness, food restriction, and purging. Engel et al. 2003 findings suggest that gender, ethnicity, sport, self-esteem, and attitudes are related to the behaviors and attitudes of disordered eating in elite athletes. As a secondary finding, Engel et al. found 81% of women and 45% of males felt out of control during a binge

episode. Among this sub-population, the male athletes tended

to not consider their binging behaviors problematic. In Johnson

et al.'s (2004) follow-up study of Engel et al.'s 2003 research,

low self-esteem was also identified as a primary risk factor in

the development of eating disorders. Within the study, a strong

correlation between eating disorders and low self-esteem and

low body dissatisfaction was established. This finding is in

support of the research findings of Garner (1991), Johnson and

Maddi (1986) and Thompson (1999).

Engel et al.'s 2003 finding of 40.5% to 46.4% is

considerably higher than the current national statistics of

anorexia and bulimia combined. Engel et al. (2003) concluded

that competitive college athletes in American colleges and

universities demonstrate many disordered eating patterns as

nearly half of the 1,445 sampled displayed disordered eating

and exercising behaviors. Furthermore, the study found higher

occurrences of eating disorder behaviors within Division I sports

than in Divisions II and III colleges. This finding suggests that athletic superiority and competitiveness is a strong predictor for disordered eating. The extreme attitudes and behaviors required for a high sport prowess match the personality traits of non-athlete persons with eating disorders. An entire section in this review is dedicated to this significant link between athletes and eating disorders.

The significance of Engel's results was addressed in an interview by Pauline Powers, Professor of Psychiatry at the University of South Florida, Director of the Eating Disorders at Laureate Psychiatric Clinic, and coauthor of Engel's study. Powers commented that the study established a higher prevalence of eating disorders among athletes with the highest occurrences befalling upon Division I athletes. As for the reason for this increased risk of an athletic environment, Powers states, "Athletes get a double dose: Not only are they trying to get thin because our society says you should appear thin, but the athletes also think being thinner, no matters what improves performance" (Eating Disorder Review, 1999). Yet, the most telling observation Powers held on the study was the EDNOS

prevalence,

> The DSM-IV criteria are both a blessing and a
>
> curse. A blessing because this is better for
>
> research, but also a curse because clinically a lot
>
> of people who have really severe eating
>
> disorders don't meet the DSM-IV criteria. In
>
> fact, about half of patients who come to
>
> specialty clinic don't meet the DSM-IV criteria
>
> [for anorexia or bulimia]. They are diagnosed
>
> with eating disorders not otherwise specified
>
> (EDNOS), even though they obviously have an
>
> eating disorder (Eating Disorder Review, 1999).

Similar to Engel, et al's study, Johnson, Powers, and Dick (1999)

also determined a high rate of disturbed eating among a

student-athlete sample. As 13% of their sample had a clinical

eating disorder, 35% and 38% were at-risk for developing

anorexia and bulimia, respectively. In this study, predictors did not meet the criteria for anorexia or bulimia yet may have fallen within the EDNOS category.

A study that advocated the research value of including the EDNOS category when sampling college athletes was Black et al.'s 2003 research. Using a female sample of 148 collegiate athletes, Black's research team found 18% of the sample to be anorexic or bulimic. Of the remaining 122 athletes, 65% (or 79 subjects) were diagnosis as EDNOS - more than doubling the "popular" anorexia and bulimia categories. Black et al. accounts for the high occurrence of eating disorders (105 subjects in a 148 person sample) in the telling statement below that strengthens that argument of including the EDNOS category for an increased validity in eating disorder research.

Prevalence rates in the present study may be higher because 'not otherwise specified' [disordered eating] were included. Otherwise, the rates of anorexia nervosa and bulimia nervous are similar to those studies by other authors (Black et al, 2003, p. 7).

In Black's 2003 research, several eating disorder behaviors were identified in a sample population of 695 male and female college athletes. A third of the sample reported a preoccupation with food; a quarter binged at least once per week; 15% held a distorted image of their body; 12% feared losing control when eating; 12% fasted for more than a day after a binge episode; 5.5% vomited to improve their mood; 5% ate until they were beyond full and nauseated; 4% abused laxatives; and 1.5% used enemas as a purging method.

In a study designed exclusively for males with an eating disorder clinic, Carlat, Camargo, and Herzog (1997) found 32% of their sample met the EDNOS diagnosis criteria, a figure 10% higher than Mitchell's 1986 study of EDNOS females. Carlat, Camargo, and Herzog (1997) concluded their study by advocating for increased research on both the male population and the EDNOS category. In the discussion of their findings, the authors stated the EDNOS classification is of great significance of study for the male population.

As the EDNOS category encompasses many facets of disturbed eating and exercise behaviors, Garman, Hayduk, Crider, and Hodel (2004) explored exercise dependency as a popular form of purging among college populations with EDNOS. The authors of this study defined exercise dependency as an over-commitment, obligatory, or compulsion of exercise without consideration of the activity's nature and intensity. From a sample of 257 college students, the researchers determined that almost 22% were "exercise dependent" - the majority of whom were male. The researchers identified 53% of the exercise dependent population also suffered from "problem eating" – or formally disordered eating. A significant number of the exercise dependent population also had disturbed body images. In parallel with eating disorder symptomology, the "problem eating" population scored high on isolation and depression scales as exercise held precedence over social invitations and obligations. With this disturbed sense of prioritization, the exercise dependent sample struggled academically as they reported time spent exercising held precedence over class preparation and attendance. With this, these pathological exercisers might very well be classified with EDBT from their obligatory and compulsive exercise behaviors.

In Garman, Hayduk, Crider, and Hodel's study, "anorexic symptoms" were not a diagnosis of anorexia. Rather, individuals who scored high on the researcher's instrument were labeled as "problem eaters" (disordered eating). It is likely that a percentage of eating disorders would have been increased if these "problem eaters" were measured for EDNOS. The authors stated their sample "may have disturbed eating attitudes and behaviors, but not necessarily clinical anorexia nervosa" (p. 629). Unfortunately, the authors only indicated their study yielded probable EDNOS outcomes within their non-classifications of anorexia. This conclusion leads one to believe that disorder eating attitudes and behaviors is an indication for a degree of EDNOS occurrences.

Even as new research is published with strikingly high findings on EDNOS prevalence rates, most researchers still ignore their peer findings by solely controlling for anorexia and bulimia. As an example of many, Stoutjesdyk and Jevne's 1993 study claimed, "the two most common forms of eating disorders are anorexia and bulimia" (p. 7). Although the popular opinion would substantiate this claim, it is false and only serves to promote eating disorders myths and male hesitancy.

Limitations of Eating Disorder Research

A brief search of eating disorder literature will reveal the domination of scholarly publications and research on anorexic and bulimic females. The rationale for this disparity is caused from a significant increased prevalence rate in females. National statistics report only one million American males are diagnosed, a figure ten times less than the female population. Within this population of males, it is estimated that 15% are bulimic and 5% anorexic. Indications suggest an increased rate of eating disorders in the form of EDNOS. Yet, the fact that eating disorders may be unrecognized in up to 50% of cases and the limited research on EDNOS and males has contributed to a lower than actual rate of occurrence (Becker, Keel, Anderson-

Fye & Thomas, 1999). One must assume a considerable amount

of males, either misdiagnosed or undetected, fall into the

EDNOS yet they are not accounted for in eating disorder

statistics. Consequently, there are fewer studies on this

population that is less affected.

With this argument considered, further reasons for the

low male diagnosis rate exists. From the research available, the

cause is threefold: 1) failure of male self-reporting from a lack of

public knowledge and popular society stigmas and myths that

promote misinformation, ignorance, and embarrassment; 2)

lack of male diagnosis from physicians due to the difficulty of

clear symptoms; and 3) the medical community's unawareness

of the EDNOS category for possible diagnosis of males exhibiting

disordered eating behaviors but not meeting anorexia or

bulimia criteria. All three disease categories take many forms

besides disordered eating: avoidance of social functions,

compulsive exercising, ritualistic and perfectionist behaviors,

etc. Besides the well-known anorexia and bulimia categories,

the third classification is of great significance for future research. EDNOS is possibility the most serious advancement of eating disorder etiology to lessen the bias among genders. Although limited in empirical research, there is a strong promise for increased male identification in studies that consider the EDNOS category. With this, it is reasonable to expect increased male prevalence rates would begin to satisfy the existing literary void by adding credibility to males with the disease and support a standard EDNOS inclusion to achieve a reasonable degree of validity in future studies.

This review contains extensive literary evidence to substantiate the unjust social and medical restrictions on males with eating disorders. The reader will also find this situation to be scholastically unjust as educational research dominates the literature with restricted studies on both classifications and genders. Few studies include the EDNOS category, yet if the category is included it often produces results of great significance to the field. Studies that have controlled for this category yielded results of a thirty-five to sixty-five occurrence rate. The social and educational irresponsibility of excluding the largest eating disorder category, one in which most males fall, only perpetuates a false understanding of eating disorders and promotes the existing myths and stigmas that discourage men from seeking treatment for this "female disease." Within this review, a thorough exploration of the disease shall clarify the discrepancies of popular perceptions and define the complex realism of the disease in an attempt to advance an accurate understanding of the illness beyond a superficial appreciation.

The above problem cause limited scholarship and advances the social ignorance of the disease. The limited inclusion of the EDNOS category is illogical and irresponsible for the presumably largest classification of eating disorders to be repeatedly excluded in scientific studies. This neglect causes invalid prevalence rates among males. This male under-representation often leads to a deepened severity of symptoms, feelings of shame, and absent treatment. With this considered, it is reasonable to theorize the reported 10% of American males with an eating disorder is a grossly underestimated figure. The deficiency of inclusive surveying aggravates the existing ignorance of males of eating disorders. By their lack an EDNOS inclusion, academia has contributed to society's bias of eating disorders. Philosophically, this has results in eating disordered males to suffer with delayed or absent diagnoses or treatment.

Since one traumatic experience in a predisposed person can trigger disordered eating behaviors, the diverse sources of pressures on the college student-athlete (coaches, teammates, peers, family, and mostly themselves) to be "perfect" is often the tipping point for the development of an eating disorder (Hausenblas & Carron, 1999). It is to this parallel of athletic participation and eating disorders that is now discussed.

The Eating Disorder–Athlete Connection

"There is a thin line between being an athlete and being anorexic" (Person, Benson-Quaziena, & Rogers, 2001, p. 57).

Research on the positive relationship between athletes and eating disorders has grown significantly since its philosophical inception. In this time, researchers that controlled for athletic participation within eating disorder studies delivered historic results. Consequently, sport participation became an area of concern, particularly at the varsity level on college campuses. The intensity of diverging pressures in an inherently competitive environment raises the occurrence of eating disorders among sport participants (Black, 1991). National expert Ron Thompson remarked, "Athletes are a special group of patients. They experience the same pressures as non-athletes and more" (Cruse, 2003). This relationship has gained enormous research backing with findings so strong that experts have labeled athletes as "at-risk" and called for a standardized eating disorder screening test designed specifically for athletes (Black, Larkin, Coster, & Leverenz, 2003).

Within the realm of sports, athletes are socially permitted to engage in and display eating disorder behaviors. Athletes tend to view losing weight as a performance enhancer (Davis, 1992; Rosen, McKeag, Hough, & Curley, 1986). The normative behaviors of rigid eating and compulsive exercise to enhance one's performance is often expected and even revered - particularly among competitive leagues. As patterns of pathogenic and maladaptive weight control measures are introduced and learned early, they evolve into an accepted part of the sport (Williamson, et al., 1995). Success in the competitive sports environment permits, encourages, and requires control over body and mind. The mastery of perfectionist qualities is valued: high achievement, intense motivation, obsessive behaviors, and attention to detail (Ludwig, 1996). The most noteworthy aspect of these traits is their daunting parallel to eating disorder traits - the same qualities encouraged for athletic success demands the integration and mastery of core eating disorder behaviors. Yet, in the athletic environment, these behaviors often pass without alarm. As these core behaviors are embedded in the world of sport competition, the athlete's involvement in their sport's preparatory behaviors will produce allegiance, devotion, esteem, and identity. These features become intertwined in the sport, creating a strong belief in the sport's normative behaviors without regard for the potential risk.

Because of these beliefs, eating disordered athletes often resist attempts to regulate or normalize their abnormal eating and exercise patterns. This apprehension may be most evident from the fear of declining performance or body shape. However, the stronger underlying emotions come from the fears of losing fulfillment, identification, and esteem. The fear of losing these qualities is the same for non-athletes that suffer from eating disorders. Because sports can be a strong aspect of an athlete's identity and self-worth, increasing this source of esteem requires a resolute commitment to the sport's normative behaviors. As individual and team behaviors contribute in forming the athlete's identity, recovery becomes complex as eating disordered athletes must refute their sport's behaviors that yielded their successes. Abandoning trusted behaviors will result in the reduction or loss of the athlete's self-identity, worth, and esteem that was provided in their involvement in the sport's culture.

Athletic involvement only further complicates the detection of an eating disorder, particularly with the male athlete. Fueled by its adoration of the male athlete, Western society's ideals calls for athletes to display specific body sizes and shapes to best represent their chosen sport. Adhering to these expected body types hinders the identification of eating disorders (Thompson & Sherman, 2001). A common interference is accepting the athlete's dietary and exercise disciplines. Indeed, many behaviors, or variations of them indicate an eating disorder even as it accounts for athletic success. This blurred impression breads a fundamental difficulty in distinguishing between an eating disorder and a dedicated athlete (Thompson & Sherman, 2001).

Despite the increased volume of information and educational efforts by governing agencies, there has not been any evidence that the presence of eating disorders in athletes has declined. Conversely, topical research has shown an upward trend. Even with findings of athletes with eating disorders mounting, many physicians and psychologists are inept to recognize and treat the intricacies held by this population

(Thompson & Sherman, 2001). To help correct this void, eating

disorder professionals have deliberately published articles to

educate the medical community on the complexities of athletes

with eating disorders.

The parallel between eating disorders and athlete

qualities was best articulated in a 1999 study by Ron Thompson

and Roberta Sherman. In their study, *"Good Athlete" Traits and

Characteristics of Anorexia Nervosa: Are They Similar?* the

authors drew upon six traits from anorexia literature and

compared them with literature on the athlete and the athletic

environment. As eating disorders are believed a significant

problem for athletes, Thompson and Sherman reaffirmed

aspects that increase an athlete's risk, but also make

identification of athletes difficult.

Thompson and Sherman referenced Yates, Leehey, and

Shisslak's then controversial 1983 study that implied obligatory

runners held comparable traits and behaviors of anorexics.

These traits included perfectionism, tendencies toward

depression, and preoccupations with body weight, rigid dieting, and exercising to compensate for overeating. Although their findings were contested by Blumenthal, O'Toole and Chang in 1984, and Rosen and Leitenberg in 1988, Yates, et al's research began to stimulate research that further examined the relationship of athletes and disordered eating behaviors.

Although many studies have found a correlation between athletes and disordered eating, the specific cause has remained undetermined. Like many of their peers, Thompson and Sherman proposed the similarity in characteristics are the foundation to this parallel. Their premise does not imply "good athletes" are pathologically associated with anorexia; rather, some of the characteristics associated with anorexia are found among these "good athletes" and are also partly responsible for their athletic successes. This belief is shared by Yates (1996) and Zerbe (1993) suggesting the shared personality traits and dedication to obligatory exercise among athletes serves to mask their eating disordered behaviors. Thompson and Sherman relied upon Oglivie's 1968 study that identified personality characteristics associated with a "good athlete" - such as emotional stability, tough mindedness, conscientiousness, self-control, low tension, extroversion, and trust.

The first similarity in Thompson and Sherman's study is "Mental Toughness / Asceticism." From the literature, the authors determined that successful athletes are unaffected by stressful situations, as they routinely make decisions in difficult conditions that are consistent with a game plan. This ability to override their emotions is a positive trait in an athletic environment. Anorexics commonly ignore their needs (hunger and pain) and practice self-denial. Furthermore, anorexics sacrifice - mostly their quality of life and health. Thompson and Sherman define "asceticism" as the "strong tendency to seek virtue through self-restraint, self-discipline, self-denial, and control of bodily urges" (2000, p. 185). In the realm of sports, sacrificing for the team's benefit and "playing with pain" are valued. As such, an anorexic athlete will appear to be tough-minded with a high degree of self-control and willpower.

The second similarity, "Commitment to Training /
Excessive Exercise" indicates the "good athlete's" ability to train
intensely – a maximal effort. Likewise, anorexics exercise
excessively in spite of psychological and physical costs.
Anorexics are known for their ability to welcome restlessness,
capitalizing the opportunity to be active. This obligatory
behavior is derived from the relief of depression that exercise
provides. With the athletes and anorexic's need for approval
and quality of being over-compliant, both populations tend to
over-train in an attempt to please a coach or improve
performance. The behavior of intense and excessive behaviors
may also originate from the athletes and anorexic's high
expectations for achievement and perfectionism. This desire for
enhanced performance serves as another rationalization for
compulsive exercise.

The third similarity of "Pursuit of Excellence /
Perfectionism" is a common anorexic quality that is revered in
the competitive sport's environment. It has been reported that
anorexics seldom feel "good enough" and therefore often worry

about rejection. Consequently, they are driven by their anxiety and fears along with their need to please and be perfect. Likewise, athletes are "determined to do their best – no matter what" (Orlick, 1990, p. 9). Athletes are traditionally conscientious, determined, and unsatisfied with their current achievements.

The willingness to be "coachable" and over-compliant is Thompson and Sherman's fourth similarity. Both athlete and anorexic have a strong need to please and / or a fear of disappointing others. Anorexics typically conform because of their need for approval. The fifth similarity is "Unselfishness / Selfishness." The quality of the unselfish athlete is a widely accepted cliché in sports. An athlete's conformity allows individual needs to be subordinate to the team. Anorexics seldom make a decision based on their needs or wants; rather the decision is superseded by their perception of the desires of others. Anorexics fear responding to his or her own needs as this may lead to conceit or rejection. This aspect of anorexia originates from the lack of responsiveness to their needs in addition to the need to please to maintain self-worth. Because

of this extrinsic motive, anorexics often have a small sense of

self. In the athletic environment, "good athletes" must put the

needs of others before their own. In doing so, athletes become

accustom to sacrificing for the "good of the team." With value

place on athletic sacrifice, this quality becomes an

acknowledgment for self-worth.

The sixth and final similarity by Thomson and Sherman

is "Performance Despite Pain / Denial of Discomfort." Pain is an

accepted and even a glorified aspect of sports. The high

tolerance of athletes with pain is a "requirement of the sport, a

badge of commitment, the test of a true athlete" (Yates, 1991,

p. 150). In Wittig and Schurr (1994), Hughes and Coakley

declared that being an athlete means "making sacrifices for the

game, striving for distinction, accepting the risks and playing

through the pain, and refusing to accept limits in the pursuit of

possibilities" (p. 328). These qualities are very similar to the

anorexic that will exercise excessively, without regard for their

level of strength or mental state.

The parallels discussed by Thompson and Sherman are found frequently among athletes as they are revered and encouraged. These personality traits, or the variation of them, are the foundation for the established link among athlete and eating disorder. Furthermore, these "good athlete" traits serve to mask eating disordered behaviors and often misinterpreted by clinicians. This, and the athletic body stereotype, contributes to the low detection rate among males, as at-risk athletes are difficult to diagnose because they display symptoms that are socially revered and enable them to perform at a superior level.

As body weight loss or gain is a critical and necessary element in the preparation and success in several sports, most athletes have a profound awareness of their body weight and shape (Baer, Walker, & Grossman, 1995). For this reason, a preoccupation of disordered eating and exercise behaviors are common in a sport's culture. To intervene with an athlete's training or dietary routine is to challenge long held beliefs that truthfully did enhance performance and aided in attaining a particular body shape. Because of the true value eating disorder behaviors has on athletic successes, it is not surprising that a 1995 study found one in five college student-athletes met the criteria for bulimia and one in thirty-three for anorexia (Burches-Miller & Black, 1995). With the recent surfacing of EDNOS and sub-clinical disordered eating and EDBT research, findings of higher prevalence rates have originated from these criteria that is more accommodating to athletes in their consideration of extreme athletic behaviors.

Because athletes share these traits, they are two to three times more likely to develop an eating disorder (Black, 1991). Although the majority of eating disorder research on athletes is female focused, the core personality traits of eating disorders and athletic preparation are shared among genders (Benson, et al., 1990; Moriarty & Moriarty, 1994). As outlying traits may differ among studies, the core traits are the same: intense discipline, underlying anxiety, strong need to excel, perfectionism, fear of maturity, intense focus on body image, undue concern for adult opinions, and self-worth linked to external validation (Black, 1991; Garner & Garfinkel, 1980).

Research on Athlete's Increased Risk

"Guys are so territorial. You go into the weight room and everyone's eyeing each other. You see a difference between the way your body looks during season and out of season."
Comment by an out of season bulimic male wrestler at Princeton University (Graham, 2004).

Although drug and alcohol abuse are the most publicized student-athlete infractions and featured headline at the institutional level, a survey by the NCAA's division of sports-science found that eating disorders have quietly become a growing issue among their populace (Dick, 1990). Randall W. Dick, Director of Sports Sciences for the NCAA, commented that the higher prevalence rates among females are comparable to reports of eating disorders in other populations. However, Dick also noted the NCAA study acknowledged a male prevalence and reasserted that eating disorders are not exclusive to the female genders by stating, "eating disorders are a complex problem often hidden by those suffering from it, no sport should be considered 'exempt' from the problem" (Dick, 1990, p. 1).

A finding of the study revealed that at least one student-athlete was found to have an eating disorder in each of the NCAA member institutions that responded to the voluntary survey (64%). The great majority of the illness (93%) was found in women's sports with women's gymnastics holding the largest percentage of eating disorders (52 reports out of 108 sponsoring schools – 48%). The next highest percentages were in women's cross-country (23%); women's swimming, not including diving (21%); and women's track and field events (21%). Women's cross-country had with the most reports with 146. Wrestling was the men's sport with both the most reports at twenty, and the greatest percentage of eating disorders (7%) among responding schools. Men's cross-country was second in both categories, with 17 reports (3%) of eating disorders from 664 sponsoring schools.

Mounting research with convincing findings led the medical community to place male and female athletes as a high-risk population for developing eating disorders (Davis, Kennedy, Ravelski, & Dionne 1994; Garner, Rosen & Barry, 1998; Kleifield,

Wagner, & Halmi, 1996; Skolnick, 1993; DePalma, Koszewski, &

Romani, 2002; Thiel, Gotfried, & Hesse, 1993). In a 2002 study

that predicted the risk of disturbed eating among a college

athlete sample, DePalma, Koszewski, and Romani (2002)

established in their study, *Identifying College Athletes at Risk for*

Pathogenic Eating, that college athletes are "particularly

susceptible to the dangers of eating disorders" (p. 45). These

sorts of speculations among theorists led to a trend of studies in

the late 1980s and 1990s intended to identify the origin of the

increased risk inherent to athletes.

The philosophy of athletic participation in eating

disorder scholarship is the shared traits that connect both

populations. Evidently, the athlete's inherent risk is a derivative

of applying eating disorder behaviors to manage the pressures

of the competitive athletic environment (Borgen & Corbin,

1987, Gardner & Garfinkel, 1980, Stoutjesdyk & Jevne, 1993).

Picard was among the first to study the shared traits of eating

disorders and athletic involvement in his 1986 study, identifying

the communal traits that placed athletes at a higher risk. The shared traits found in Picard's study were high self-expectations; a rigid and obsessive approach to goal obtainment; perfectionist mannerisms; pressure to excel; a high emphasis on emotional control; high levels of competitiveness, compulsiveness, drive for success, self-motivation; heightened body awareness; and a propensity to self-deprive and isolate. The parallels established in Picard's study spawned future research that led the medical community to identify athletes as a high-risk population for developing eating disorders (Borresen-Gresko & Karlenson, 1994); Rosen & Gross, 1987; Stoutjesdyk and Jevne, 1993). Yeager, Agostini, Nattiiv, and Drinkwater (1993) were among the researchers that further studied these common traits. In his study, Yeager reported that when focused on the body, these traits will most likely lead to disordered eating behaviors. In agreement with peer research, Yeager also determined the traits that enhance athletic prowess are the foundation of an eating disorder. Theorists trust this relationship predisposes athletes, and therein lays the increased risk.

As noted, athletes often maintain a heightened sense of body awareness, a quality whose likelihood increases with the athlete's level of competition. These athletes often have unrealistic performance expectations of themselves and others. In spite of their many achievements, they may feel inadequate, defective, and worthless. In many cases, these athletes see their world as black and white; everything is good or bad, a success or a failure - a win or a loss. These competitive athletes are also more prone to have the shared eating disorder traits of perfectionism, compulsiveness, overachievement, strict discipline, and high self-expectations (Garner and Garfinkel, 1980; Taub and Blinde, 1992; Thornton, Leo, Alberg, 1991; Yates, Leehey & Shisslak, 1983). These traits are advantageous, perhaps necessary to enhance athletic performance. The dangers of these qualities are often overlooked due to their acceptance in athletics. Mastering these traits to a high degree in athletics is revered and even considered a source of disciplinary pride. Ironically, the same traits viewed as essential and respected in athletics are notoriously and deeply allied with eating disorders.

Driven athletes increase their level of risk by upholding a strong control over their body shape, weight, and strength to improve sport performance. In 2001, Krane, Waldron, Stiles-Shipley and Michalenok found 44.6% of their student-athlete female sample engaged in additional exercise beyond team requirements. This behavior constitutes a risk of developing an eating disorder through compulsive exercising. With a disquieting irony, attempts to obtain a higher level of athletic performance are often benefited by adhering to eating disorder behaviors. The shared behaviors and beliefs that tie athletes to eating disorders is the need for control, as control sustains the need for the disease. Experts that have studied this correlation cite the athlete's tendency to control for unreasonably high self-expectations. When these expectations are unmet, the control over one's self is intensified in a reattempt to achieve the goal (Anderson, Bartlett, Morgan, & Rowena, 1995).

Founder and President of the Eating Disorder Center at
Harvard University, David Herzog, identified a possible
physiological cause for the increased rate of eating disordered
behaviors among athletes. Researching brain functioning lead
Herzog to discover a decrease in body weight will causes the
brain to shrink. The decrease in brain size will constricted one's
ability to thinking clearly. In unison, the athlete's customary
practices of dieting, exercise, and at times purging will release
endorphins and opioids into the body. These chemicals cause a
temporary addictive feeling of euphoria. With an unclear
thought process and craving for spurts of euphoria, an addictive
progression is the likely result that may lead to a cycle of
pathogenic eating and exercise. In similar research, Katz's 1986
study found extreme exercise to advance the onset of eating
disorders. Katz's finding is based in human biology and social
reinforcement that often follows a weight loss. As body weight
decreases, Katz identified a diminished appetite, increased
narcissistic investment in one's body, and elevated level of
endorphins that enhance mood.

Even as a substantial portion of eating disorder etiology has linked the disease to familial, sociocultural and bio-psychological factors, the identification these diverging underlying causes have not distinguished a single central core reason that validates the increased risk of athletic participation. Hoping to better define this link among athletes, several scholars adhere to the subsequent theories: 1) predisposing personality characteristics shared among eating disorders leads to athletic excellence and disordered eating; 2) participation in particular sports (lean-type, weight restrictive, or appearance based) causes self-consciousness and adoption of cultural norms; and 3) a predisposition to eating disorders and therefore an attraction to lean-type sports to justify behaviors. (Cullari, Rohrer, & Bahm, 1998; Graber & Brooks-Gunn, 1996; Noles, Cash, & Winstead, 1995; Sokol, Steinberg, & Zerbe, 1998; Kirk, Singh, & Getz, 2002).

A combination of the three premises would be the likely reasons for the increase in risk. Regardless of the most accepted argument, the core factor of any population with eating disorders is a lack of control, perceived or otherwise. It is this constant that binds all populations regardless of gender, race, social economical class, or leisure pursuit. This eating disorder feature is critical to note, as it is the grounding presupposition and underlying premise for all eating disorder research and theory.

While a specific origin has not been pinpointed, the research is very clear that higher athletic competition will increase the eating disorder risk (APA, 1994). Without substantial opposition, most theorists agree that a high level of competition will produce higher degrees of control over the shared traits in predisposed athletes. Research has validated higher occurrences of eating disorders amid more competitive leagues. With this, theorists have shown significant increases of athletes with eating disorders that participate in Division I college leagues as opposed to those in that inhabit Division II or III conferences.

Amid the inflicted pressures inherent to student-athletes, one's own ambition for superior performance and a high team ranking can become a trigger for developing

pathogenic eating disorder behaviors. In a study on the

lifestyles and consequential health risks of college athletes,

Nattiv and Puffer (1991) identified an elevated risk for eating

disorder behaviors among elite (Division I-A) levels of

competition. The authors reported that the demanding lifestyle

of a Division I student-athlete added a substantial amount of

emotional, physical, and mental pressure that resulted in higher

percentages of maladaptive eating and exercising behaviors

(Nattiv & Puffer, 1991). Nattiv and Puffer's premise was based

on the underlining theory within Black and Burckes-Miller's

1988 research that found student-athlete's risk is two to three

times higher risk for developing a clinical eating disorder than

their non-athlete college peers.

The external and internal stressors of participating in

college athletics often yields a more cautious student-athlete in

their body size and shape. Causing much confusion among ill

student-athletes, the traits that increase an athlete's

vulnerability to the disease are the same traits that are

beneficial and rewarded in sports. This divergence can cause a great degree of uncertainty for the athlete and ambiguity in identifying the eating disorder. Although it is not proven as a direct path to a diagnosis, these discernible stressors may predispose an athlete to employ an undue and inordinate amount of controls that support the developing illness. These additional pressures often cause athletes to shift the focus of their control on rigorous means to dictate their body weight or shape. Restrictive caloric intake and excessive exercise may not initially hinder the athletes' performance, but ultimately their ability to function will decline. Yet, even as athletic performance suffers, the addictive cyclical nature of their routine – their eating disorder - causes predisposed athletes to continue their maladaptive behaviors even as their athletic performance suffers.

Within this context of multiple sources of pressures on a student-athlete, Krane, Waldron, Stiles-Shipley, and Michalenok's 2001 study identified self-presentation as a dominating aspect in the culture of collegiate sports. Krane et al. (2001) defined self-presentation as peers evaluating one's physique and skill level. Often in males, the shift from exercising and eating to improve personal health is quickly turned to changing one's physique for external approval. It is within this transitional change in motivation that one becomes far more susceptible to adopt eating disorder behaviors to attain a specific appearance. As this 'ideal' physique evolves into a more specific look, the inaccessibility of the unattainable can evolve into a perpetuating drive for "success" that positions one to developing an eating disorder (Krane, Waldron, Stiles-Shipley, & Michalenok, 2001).

Self-presentation as the value placed on an athletic physique was measured in Leary and Kowalski's 1990 research. The authors learned that social status in the culture of American colleges is largely obtained by one's physical appearance and social associations. In accord with Leary and Kowalski's findings, Hausenblas and Mack's 1999 study found participation in college athletics was a direct increase of the student's cultural capitol: status, influence, and impressions. Among his findings,

Mack discovered that student-athletes with an aesthetic physique were rated favorably on 19 of the 20 dimensions of status that were measured. Mack concluded that the pressure on student-athletes to uphold their high status can become a profound affliction, leading to an increase in eating disorders to obtain some sense of privacy and control.

Specific to anorexia, Slavin (1987) noted that female athletes and anorexics share more than personality traits. In this study, Krane use a scientific instrument to measure the degree of correlation between perfectionism and drive for thinness. With this instrument, his female athlete sample scored unusually high. This exploratory study found common fixations of dietary faddism, controlled calorie intake, carbohydrate avoidance, low body weight, abnormally slow resting heart rate, and amenorrhea. Slavin's study also upheld the shared perfectionist traits and reported another - the psychological comfort of hiding one's body by wearing baggy, lose-fitting clothing.

As a precursor to Engel' et al.'s 2003 landmark study,

Striegel-Moore and Smolak (2001) reported a strong connection

between elite athletic involvement and disordered eating.

Hausenblaus and Carron found the same coloration in their

1999 study, as did Sundgot-Borgen in her 1999 study. As noted

in all three studies, by a future survey of the sample, the

researchers determined their student-athlete sample had a

significant degree of under-reporting of their disordered eating

pathology. This discovery negatively affected the study's

reported rates of prevalence.

In 2003, Black, Larkin, Coster, Leverenz, and Abood

developed an instrument to measure eating disorders among

female athletes. Their motive for creating this tailored

assessment instrument was the high number of athletes that

displayed eating disorder behaviors but were not diagnosed

with conventional eating disorder assessment instruments.

Even as athletes are diagnosed at a rate up to three times

higher than non-athletes, Black et al.'s study determined their

extreme behaviors may not always meet the DSM-IV's strict

criteria. Besides not meeting the medical criteria, the study

indicated that the perception of an athlete's preparatory

behaviors as a normal, voluntary aspect of their sport leads to

the athlete remaining undetected. As Black's research team

tested their instrument on a female college athlete sample, one

out of three respondents was identified as having disordered

eating. The sample's high occurrence rate of pathogenic weight

control behaviors was supported by Black's earlier study in 1991

and with Burckes-Miller's study in 1988. Black, Larkin, Coster,

Leverenz, and Abood's 2003 study advocated the inclusion of

the EDNOS category in future eating disorder research. The

authors feared a significant portion of athletes suffers from

eating disorders, yet they are not statistically represented or

medically treated.

Accepting researchers' counsel regarding the EDNOS

category, the American College of Sports Medicine included the

category in their study prompted by the increased occurrences

of disordered eating in college athletics. By measuring for

EDNOS, this study was able to best evaluate the maladaptive

tendencies of some athletes. Consequently, a 62% prevalence

rate among female college athletes was found. Notably, this

statistic is considerably greater than the 10% national average

for females. Also finding a high prevalence rate, Rosen and

McKeag (1986) reported 36% of surveyed collegiate female

athlete participants held at least one pathogenic behavior of an

EDNOS diagnosis. Furthermore, although 90% to 95% of

reported eating disorders are in females, Powers and Johnson

(2002) declared that when considering the EDNOS category,

male athletes are "at least equally at risk" (p. 7).

At the 2002 conference of the American Psychological

Association, a study presented by Ohio State University

reported finding one in six college athletes were diagnosed with

disordered eating. Although not as significant as this occurrence

ratio, the study found 15% of Ohio State's student-athletes

were anorexic or bulimic. A statement by Jennifer Carter, the

lead researcher and sport psychologist at Ohio State,

commented, "The fittest people on campus are probably this

group of student-athletes, but many of them thought they had too much fat in some areas" (Carter, 2002). In this study of 680

Ohio State student-athletes (34 varsity sports: 17 male and 17

female) 20% of the female athletes and 15% of male athletes

displayed eating disorder characteristics. By comparing the

eating disorder rates found in earlier studies of 19% to 32%

among non-athletes, Carter felt her institution's athletes were

not at an increased risk. However, Carter (2002) admitted

disappointment in the reported negative body images by her

university's athletes, an aspect of the study she justified by

claiming athletes are "perfectionists and that includes

perfecting their physique." This survey was conducted to

restructure Ohio State's policies on student-athletes with eating

disorders. It is important to note that the validity of this survey

is questionable since the student's anonymity was not

maintained. Prior to taking the survey, students were notified

that their coaches would be informed of any reported eating

disorder behaviors. If reported the athlete was aware they

would receive mandatory counseling by the Ohio State

psychology center.

Among the research on college athletes and eating disorders, one must consider Stoutajesdyk and Jevne's 1993 study of 277 male and female student-athletes that participated in lean and weight-restrictive sports among fourteen Division I-A institutions. Selected sports were included based on studies that had shown the highest prevalence rates of anorexia and bulimia. In this study, Stoutajesdyk and Jevne measured the athletes' eating behaviors and their corresponding emotions. The study findings revealed anorexic diagnoses in 10.6% of their female sample and 4.6% in the male population – a ratio among genders much closer than the national average.

With the theoretical view that individuals preoccupied with appearance and weight are inclined to use sports to pacify and conceal their desires, a recent 2002 study by Powers and Johnson cited numerous studies in support of this view. By surveying college athletes, it was revealed that male athletes' preferred method of purging was excessive sauna or steam bath use. They further established that increased physical activity will decrease an appetite. This chemical change will frequently result in a weight loss. Notably, Powers and Johnson (2005) claim that college athletes are often aware of their disordered eating behaviors, but do not seek treatment for fear of being forced to stop participating in their sport.

In 2002, Powers and Johnson also gave testament to research that advocated eating disorders as a significant problem in college athletics. The authors claimed the increased risk originates from sports that emphasize a thin body or an idyllic figure (gymnastics, ballet, figure skating, swimming, distance running). Powers and Johnson also contend that participating in wrestling and bodybuilding pose a considerable risk for males. The authors cited research alleging a greater risk for eating disorders in sports that perform anaerobic activities as opposed to aerobic exercise. Similar results were found in Skolnick's 1993 study that reported "seriously abnormal eating patterns" in almost 16% of female college swimmers and 62% of college gymnasts (1993, p. 270). In Thiel, Gottfried, and Hesse (1993), 11% of male rowers and wrestlers were identified as having an eating disorder.

Abuse of appetite suppressants, stimulants, laxatives, and diuretics were found in Johnson's 1994 study on college athletes. Higher prevalence of abuse was shown among collegiate gymnasts, dancer, figure skating, and cross-country runners. Rosen and Hough's 1998 research identified 62% of their female collegiate sample of gymnasts used a minimum of one extreme weight loss method for three of more consecutive months. Weight loss methods considered extreme were self-induced vomiting (26%), diet pills (24%), diuretics (12%), and laxatives (7%).

Rosen and Hough found these rates of abuse to be much higher as compared to college students that did not participate in athletics. In a similar study by Anderson et al. (1991), diet aids were identified as the most common weight control method among female college athletes. Eleven percent of female athletes in college abused diet aides - a rate four times higher than male athletes (Anderson et al., 1991). Contradictory to these studies that found high rates of disordered eating behaviors, Heatherton, Nichols, Mahamedi, and Keel' s 1995 longitudinal study (1982-1992) revealed much lower rates of abuse among female student-athletes: self-induced vomiting (3%); laxatives abuse (1%); diuretic abuse (1%).

Black, Larkin, Coster, Leverenz, and Abood's (2003) research found incidences of anorexia, bulimia, and EDNOS diagnoses in ten of twelve female sports. Thirty-one percent of the diagnoses were in sports not considered to be appearance, lean, or weight-restricted. This high prevalence of eating disorders in a variety of sports was most likely produced by the inclusion the EDNOS category. Two studies authored by DePalma upheld the need for future studies to include the EDNOS category. DePalma' et al.'s earlier study in 1993 found 11% of college football players were at a significant risk for developing an eating disorder. Moreover, 52% of these *football players* (a sport not traditional considered in eating disorder studies as players are view to epitomize the opposite of eating disordered behaviors) displayed "dysfunctional eating behaviors" (DePalma et al., 1993). This study reinforces the understudied areas of eating disorders and the ignorance maintained through their exclusion.

DePalma, Koszewski, and Romani's 2002 study further substantiated and advanced DePalma's 1993 findings. By surveying 746 college male and female student-athletes in a cross-section of sports from Division I, II, and III institutions, DePalma, Koszewski, and Romani found 70% of the student-athletes were considered high risk in developing dysfunctional eating behaviors. This remarkable figure of disordered eating among 70% of their sample holds even more significance when considering the study's degree of confidentiality. The study's design permitted coaches to have full access to their athlete's responses – an aspect of the survey made known to the student-athletes prior to their participation. Given this low-level of confidentiality and possible perceived fear of punishment, one could assume an even higher presence of risk for dysfunctional eating existed.

Despite extensive research that linked athletes to eating disorders, some scholars argue against the belief of higher athlete prevalence. This presumption is held in the research of Slay, Hayaki, Napolitano, & Brownell (1998) and in Lindboe and Slettebo (1984). Both studies operate under the premise that an athlete's motivation to be thin is solely derived from their sport participation and the natural desire to succeed. In fact, these studies theorized that as leanness improves performance it is the athlete's single motivation to be thin. Both studies presume that anorexics do not exercise to improve athleticism, but simply to purge calories in their quest for thinness. With this premise, the researchers hypothesize that athletes cannot meet the anorexic criteria because they do not have an intense fear of becoming fat.

The counter argument to this premise is the loss of control that occurs in predisposed athletes. As the athlete is able to mold body shape and / or their performance improves, there is a natural desire to repeat and intensify their "formula of success." An athlete with obsessive tendencies will resist abandoning their maladaptive behaviors because of their primary narrow focus in obtaining a goal. For athletes possessing the shared eating disorder traits, the progression of goal attainment in one's behavioral frequency or intensity can be focal point of training. Consequently, pathogenic eating and exercise becomes all-encompassing and evolves into their goal. At this point, logic and reasoning is muted as the athlete remains intensely focused on sustaining their daily behaviors. Unfortunately, the initial purity of athlete success is a common beginning for athletes with eating disorders.

Although Slay, Hayaki, Napolitano, & Brownell (1998) and Lindboe and Slettebo (1984) research findings substantiate each other's work, both premises only consider anorexia. The studies' theory of "leanness to improve performance," although valid, changes from functional to pathogenic when the athlete's desire to be lean becomes an attractive means to control one's body size and shape. This act is easily masked in the athlete's attempt to better their performance. Specific to Lindboe and Slettebo's research conducted in 1984, the authors did not have the benefit of considering the highly credible research findings in the late 1980s and 1990s on shared traits and predisposition.

Yet, even with this in mind, it was proven and widely accepted in the early 1980s that the highest occurrences of eating disorders fall within lean-type sports (e.g., gymnastics, wrestlers, long distance runners, diving). These are the very sports that Slay, Hayaki, Napolitano and Brownell (1998) and Lindboe and Slettebo (1984) deem suitable for leanness while disregarding any propensities for eating disorders. When considering the basic principles established by research, it is reasonable to concede the initial motivation to be lean may originate from a desire to improve performance. However, with the strong competitive qualities of athletes, this motivation can develop into an addiction of control, merely cloaked by the athlete's "need" to be thin for their sport (Borgen & Corbin, 1987, Combs, 1982; Henry, 1982; Rosen & McKeag, 1986).

While scholarship on the relationship of disease and athletic participation remains strong, Mallick, Whipple, and Huerta's 1997 research identified specific differences in their sample of anorexics and anorexic athletes. The researchers attest that despite the athlete's anorexic-like behaviors, they tend to maintain a better self-image, have less intense fears of gaining body fat, and are more inclined to accurately perceive their body shape without distortion. The study's hypothesis alleges the athlete's motivation for weight loss is performance-based. This motivation is contrary to the anorexic's desire to be thin (Stoutjesdyk and Jevne, 1993). This finding suggest a difference in the psychological processes of eating disordered athletes as did the findings of Slay, Hayaki, Napolitano, & Brownell (1998); Mallick, Whipple, and Huerta (1987); and Lindboe and Slettebo (1984).

A conference presentation at the Academy for Eating Disorders in May of 2001 disputed the argument that intensive training causes athletes to be more susceptible to an eating disorder. The researchers from Toronto General Hospital and York University believe athletic involvement does not predispose an athlete from adopting eating disordered behaviors, accepting that people with eating disorders may participate in athletics, but this participation will not trigger the illness. In their presentation the authors stated,

There is little valid support for the theory that athletes with eating disorders are psychologically different from their non-athlete counterparts, nor any justification for the label of 'anorexia athletica' or 'activity anorexia' [EDBT]. There is no support for the concept that athletes with eating disorders are less ill than other eating disordered patients, or that their symptoms are simply due to overtraining and the intensive training frequently required of elite athletes.

In 2004, Johnson et al. expected to prove involvement in college athletics is a protective factor against eating disorders. However, the study's findings contradicted this hypothesis by yielding research outcomes comparable to Johnson, Powers, and Dick's 1999 research, Sungot-Borgen in 1994a and Thompson and Sherman's 1993 study. The researchers in Johnson's study observed higher prevalence rates of eating disorders in their sample of college athletes. As their study's hypothesis was unproven, the researchers noticed their data indicated participation in college athletics may increase the risk in developing an eating disorder.

The following studies serve as the minority view of theorists that oppose a link between athletes and eating disorders. The majority of studies have proven otherwise, and their findings are widely accepted in medical circles. The studies in this literature review are the most prominent research conducted on the topic of athletes and eating disorders. When fundamental eating disorder principles are considered, it is difficult and scholarly unpopular to adhere to a contradictory belief.

The research conducted by Gutesell, Moreau, and Thompson (2003) did not find elevated occurrences of eating disorders in college athletes as compared to non-athletes in college. By obtaining descriptive data from anonymous, self-report surveys, eating habits and behaviors were measured in addition to alcohol consumption and behaviors. The sample population consisted of 149 female varsity athletes and 209 female non-athletes from two NCAA Division I universities. The data collected included actual and desired weight, meal patterns, methods of gaining or losing weight, details of past or current eating problem, two-week alcohol consumption quantity and frequency, and detailed alcohol behaviors.

When the results were compared between the two groups, Gutesell, Moreau, and Thompson found non-athletes ate fewer meals, and they reported feeling that they were too heavy and lied about their weight-control practices. Neither group reported high rates of maladaptive behaviors such as vomiting. Nearly 18% of the athletes and 26% of the non-athletes reported past or current eating disorders. Furthermore, Gutesell study found that athletes did not differ from the non-athletes in their reported alcohol behaviors. This report found nearly 50% of both groups engaged in binge drinking, concluding that problem behaviors in eating and drinking existed equally in groups. The researchers presumed the similar scores of athletes was a result of the support provided by a coach, athletic trainer, or peer-group counseling. Their second assumption for this similarity was a reference to a general trend

of lower rates for unhealthy behaviors among female athletes.

In a 1992 meta-analysis by Brownwell, Rodin and

Wilmore, the researchers considered twenty-five separate

studies on athletes and the occurrences of eating disorders. This

gathering of completed research concluded that athletes

frequently eat pathogenically by their fixation on consuming

specific foods at certain time intervals; practice unhealthy

weight control measures common for a bulimic; and have an

entrenched drive for thinness. Even though these findings held

valid indications of eating disorders, the sample did not display

the high degree of behaviors needed to meet the DSM-IV's

criteria for anorexia or bulimia.

Earlier studies conducted before 1980 rarely examined

the actual prevalence of eating disorders among athletes.

Rather, most studies used female samples of athletes and

controlled for selected sports (Johnson, Powers, & Dick, 1999;

Sundgot-Borgen, 1994b). In her 1994 study, renowned eating

disorder theorist Sundgot-Borgen only found 1.3% of elite

athletes met all of the DSM-IV's criteria for an eating disorder.

Likewise, Johnson et al. (2004) reported 13% of his athlete

sample had "clinically significant problems" that did not meet

the criteria for anorexia or bulimia, but may reach a high degree

of EDNOS presence. Both Sundgot-Borgen (1994a) and Johnson

et al. (2004) admitted their findings were conservative

estimates.

The above studies that produced low eating disorder

occurrences in their results are similar in that despite their lack

of clinical diagnoses they still demonstrate disturbed eating and

exercise behaviors in the athlete sample. When the EDNOS

category is not a diagnostic option, a degree of those with

eating disorders will remain unidentified. This occurs most often

as the person displays the behavior but not at the needed

frequency. It is unfortunate that these studies' methodology is

in accord with most eating disorder research by failing to

control for EDNOS among a sample of athletes. This

classification is tailored more toward the dysfunctional

behaviors of an athlete. Needless to say, an increase presence of eating disorders would be shown if these categories were

considered.

Just as Sundot-Borgen, Johnson et al., and Brownwell

and Rodin's research methods failed to include the EDNOS

category, most other studies on the prevalence of athletes with

eating disorders did not as well (Brownell, Robin, & Wilmore

(1992): Petrie (1993); Petrie and Sherman (1999); and Petrie

(1993). Results from these studies yielded high occurrences of

athletes with eating disorder behaviors, but failed to meet the

DSM-IV's criteria causing many researchers and authors to refer

to this undiagnosed population as having "disordered eating." In

studies, this terminology refers to the section of individuals that

possess pathogenic and maladaptive eating patterns and

behaviors, but not severe or frequent enough to meet the DSM-

IVs' anorexia or bulimia criteria. Clearly, including the EDNOS

category is the responsible and necessary approach to maintain

validity of the study by producing true eating disorder

prevalence rates.

The common exclusion of this category leads to a misrepresentation of eating disorders, particularity among men and athletes. This is puzzling as EDNOS is a legitimate clinical eating disorder category. If all three clinical categories eating disorder categories were included (anorexia, bulimia, and EDNOS) in a study's design, the assumption of elevated eating disorders in males and male athletes would likely be confirmed. Since an eating disorder is comprised of three not two clinical categories, the current statistics are misleading. As a result, the medical field does not have reason to act with a sense of urgency even though males and collegiate athletes are likely suffering at an equivalent rate to the female population.

Lending credibility to this claim, Powers, Johnson, and Dick (1999) address this issue as they included the EDNOS category in their research, finding male athletes are "at least equally at risk" as females for displaying disordered eating pathology. In the following section, additional topical studies on the relationship amid eating disorders and athletes are examined.

Normative Behaviors in Sports

"We will spill - together, we will hurl. Out from the depths will cascade the very things that allow us to be: water, food, nourishment - of course; but image, identity, and ideas as well. Approach the mirror, seek the self, see the other and let the waters flow" (Velez, 2006).

Normative behaviors in athletics are often addressed in eating disorder literature. This association is worth mentioning since normative behaviors contribute to disturbed patterns of eating and exercise. This aspect of the "athlete-eating disorder" parallel has allowed common reference to three categories of sports with the highest rates of anorexia or bulimia: 1) Lean-type (e.g., cross-country), 2) Weight-Restricted (e.g., wrestling), and 3) Uniform-Revealing (e.g., swimming and diving). By their nature, sport in these categories encourage, support, or require eating disordered behaviors. Yet, participants may not be aware of their ill-association. Consequently, athletes prone to eating disorders may develop the disease from their obligation of the sport.

Some instances in sports will perpetuate a faulty environment, as a group-think (team) mentality will encourage normative behaviors. A group-think mentality often occurs as disordered behaviors become embedded into the very fabric of a sport. As a perceived necessity, members of a team may adopt extreme measures to better performance or qualify for a competition. Group-think mentalities often cause a self-perpetuating sub-culture of normative behaviors that appear "necessary" and "normal" to participate in the sport. As athletes integrate normative behaviors into their sport's regimen, they will often receive positive confirmation from unknowing coaches and teammates. Consequently, their faith in the behaviors as necessary and normal is strengthened. At this point, the behaviors have become habitual required aspects of their sport. As Alexander (1998) found disordered eating behaviors as an "effective method of weight management for athletes" (p. 8), these behaviors become a normalized part of the sport's culture. There is an insignificant amount of distress among teammates, particularly in males as they often act strong

among peers. Anderson (1995) states,

> When subgroups of males are exposed to
>
> situations requiring weight loss – such as occurs
>
> with wresters, swimmers, runners, and jockeys
>
> – then a substantial increase in the behaviors of
>
> self-starvation and / or bulimic symptomology
>
> follows, suggest that behavioral reinforcement,
>
> not gender, is the critical element (p. 7).

This detached sense of truth may cause athletes to believe the

absence of such behaviors will weaken performance and result

in team disappointment. As the participant's acceptance of the

behaviors evolve into a requirement of the sport, the athlete's

identity as a member of a team and participant of a sport

becomes solidified. As this dependence deepens, the athlete

begins adhering to an eating disorder mentality. While this

accepted wisdom is progressed, so does the degree of loyalty

and dependability of the behaviors. The facet of a group-think

mentality with normative behaviors is a complex in nature

because of the embeddings in the sport's culture. Attempted interventions, especially from non-team members, are often seen as a failure to understand the requirements needed to compete. For this reason, a team intervention is the most effective method to break the pathogenic cycle.

To further complicate this aspect of sports, many athletes report coaches advocate normative behaviors to the team. Unaware coaches can improperly pressure athletes to adopt behaviors to improve performance. The power dynamic between coach and player can quickly accelerate the athlete's motivation to control their body weight or shape to not hinder or disappoint the team. An athlete's "need to please" may prevent a disclosure for fear of upsetting a coach, losing status or playing time (Harris & Greco, 1990). A comment - direct, indirect, or perceived - can be the impetus for a predisposed athlete to begin scrutinizing their body and experimenting with weight control behaviors, ignorant to its emotional clench.

A coach or authority figure causing this cycle of pathogenic behaviors was studied by Anderson, Bowers, and

Watson in 2001. Their research findings indicated that even a casual remark by a coach can influence an athlete's behaviors and self-perception. In his study, Anderson found a high rate of athletes dieted to improve their performance based on a coach's recommendation. He also established a strong correlation between dieting at an early age and eating disorders. Anderson declared a coach's recommendation can easily be perceived as a requirement or demand. Other researchers have studied the results of comments by coaches. One study learned that 75% of female gymnasts sampled were told by their coach that they were "too heavy" for their sport. As a result, many of the gymnasts adopted unhealthy weight control behaviors.

The most influential practice that endorses normative behaviors and reinforces a group-think mentality is public weight assessments and body shape critiques. This practice may cause a considerable degree of public embarrassment, lasting feelings of inadequacy, and further advance competition among teammates to "win" by obtaining the lowest or an idyllic appearance. Within this type of environment, the underlying team and self-competition may encourage athletes to apply eating disorder behaviors in the attempt to obtain the set goal, pleasing their supposed authority.

The concept of normative behaviors in a college athletic environment was addressed in Thompson and Sherman's 1999 study that concluded these codes of behavior would contribute to disordered eating patterns among athletes. Thompson and Sherman reported that pressures from either coaches or teammates - real or imagined - can lead an athlete to accept that extreme measures are a required norm in their sport. From their study's findings, Thompson and Sherman concluded that the mere assumption of teammates utilizing any unhealthy behaviors resulted in the presumptuous athlete to score the highest among the sample in an index that measured purging.

Another finding that supports Thompson and Sherman's results is the research of Engel, et al. (2003). Engel and his research team determined the isomorphic relationship of eating disorders and the parallel perceptions of teammate behavior can be justified by two assumptions. First, the athlete's perception or rating of teammate behaviors is an accurate portrayal. A degree of the team engages in disordered eating and exercise behaviors in alliance with the sport's culture. Consequently, the likelihood of other teammates adopting the behaviors increases. In this scenario, team members may not only model but also encourage the behaviors. The second hypothesis of introducing of disordered behaviors in a team is the perception of a member overestimating the commonality of team's collective adherence to the behaviors. Krueger and Clement (1994) coined these occurrences as a "false-consensus effect." Sadly, a misperception can cause the onset of eating disorder behaviors even as the belief of patterned maladaptive behaviors is inaccurate. Again, the concept of assumptions as grounds to adopt disordered behaviors was substantiated in Thompson and Sherman's 1999 study.

Comparable to theories on motivational and group-think philosophies, a recent study by Duda, Bernadot, and Kim (2004) advised the NCAA examine the prevalence of motivational and ego-involving climates within their member institutions. In a motivational climate, athletes are rewarded for their degree of effort or personal improvement. This climate is comparable to the mission of a Division III institution, thus the lower presence of eating disorders as compared to an athletic environment of a Division I institution. Conversely, an ego-involving climate is equivalent to a group-think mentality. Favoritism is bestowed to the most talented team members; mistakes are punished and rivalry encouraged (Duda, Benardot, & Kim, 2004). It is within this type of hostile and competitive environment that self-presentation is exaggerated and unhealthy eating and exercising behaviors encouraged. The ego-involving climate tends to negatively affect body image and causes a lack of mental energy due to the diverging stressors. Duda, Bernadot, and Kim's research found the team's climate will significantly affect a student-athlete's body image. The climate created by coaches and propelled by teammates produces underlying consequences and rewards (Ames-Frenkel, et al., 1992). The 2004 Duda, Bernadot, and Kim study contended that competitive team environments occur frequently, citing that the ego-involving climate is a contributing factor for reports of Division I athletes having higher prevalence rates of eating disorders than athletes in less competitive leagues.

Sport-Specific Occurrences

"I'm an anorexic basketball player; without basketball, I'm just an anorexic." (Thompson & Sherman, 2001, p. 32).

Although the literature does not claim a casual link between athletic participation and eating disorders, many researchers have found by their very nature certain types of sports have higher occurrences of eating disorders. Disordered eating occurs in all sports, yet it is not equally distributed among them. For some athletes their eating disorder is directly related to their sport. For others, their disordered eating is unrelated to sport participation (Smolak, Murnen & Ruble, 2000). Leading researches maintain the following sports can encourage eating disorders among participants. One can observe these specific sports fall within one of the three high-

risk categories discussed in the prior section: dance (Garner,

1984; Hamilton et al., 1986; Hamilton, Brooks-Gunn, & Warren,

1986; Anthony, Wood, & Goldberg, 1982); figure skating (Perry,

1986); gymnastics (Kostar, 1983; Rosen & McKeag, 1986) middle

distance and marathon running (Katz, 1986; Yates, Leehey, &

Shisslak, 1983), and swimming, diving, rowing, riding, and

wrestling (Black & Burckes-Miller, 1988; Burches-Miller & Black,

1988; Leichner, Rallo, and Leichner, 1989; Rosen & McKeag,

1986; Holliman, 1991; and Brownell, Rodin, and Wilmore, 1992).

Eating disorders can be encouraged in sports cultures

that endorse low body fat, low or high body weights, or the

attainment of an ideal body type (Thompson & Sherman, 2001).

Besides assisting the athlete to accomplish the above physical

goals, these behaviors can help athletes to manage and alleviate

the inherent pressures and anxieties of sport competition and

performance (Thompson & Sherman, 2001). Because low-self

esteem is a basic eating disorder trait, participation in a sport

can be the ill athlete's primary, or perhaps only, source of esteem and identity. A quote from Thompson and Sherman's 2001 study touched upon the importance of sports as a source for self-esteem and identity. When an eating disordered athlete is considered, the importance of the sport can take on many meanings - "I'm an anorexic basketball player; without basketball, I'm just an anorexic" (p. 32).

Research on the early selection and training for a specifically chosen sport proved to encourage eating disorders in a sample of 522 elite female Norwegian athletes that represented six groups of sports: 1) technical, 2) endurance, 3) aesthetic, 4) weight dependent, 5) ball games, and 6) power sports. The study's findings revealed a significant number of athletes struggled to prevent or counter the natural physical changes precipitated by normal growth and maturity. The researchers found that a person's natural body type commonly steers the athlete toward a specific sport as their body type can be used as an asset for success. Training for a specific sport prior to the body's maturation can hinder athletes from selecting a sport befitting to their matured body type. As a result, the athlete may adopt an eating disorder to "fit" into the particular body shape of their sport. Coincidently, there is a correlation among pre-pubescent specific sport training and eating disorders.

From the common findings from years of research, many theorists believe athletes participating in sports that emphasize leanness (track, diving, rowing) or match opponents by weight (boxing, wrestling), have an inherent risk of eating disorder development. However, some scholars disagree. A related study on this topic is Sundgot-Borgen's research on pathogenic weight control. Sundgot-Borgen found that the nature of a sport can either prevent or predispose eating disorders. The types of sports most likely to increase the risk among participants are endurance, aesthetic, and weight dependent sports. However, certain theorists believe there is a lack of empirical evidence to suggest such a theory. These scholars adhere to the philosophy that specific sports do not persuade athletes to be body weight or food fixated (Black et al., 2003; Davis & Cowles, 1989; Rogers, Petrie & Trent 1996;

Sundgot-Borgen, 1994). This opposing theory is grounded in the

presumption that all athletes' performance would benefit from

increased leanness and muscularity, thus their desire of

obtainment. This assumption relies on the causation of eating

disorders, that is, predisposed individuals have a sense of losing

control, whether derived from the culture of a sport or personal

hardships. Yet, it is widely accepted that the nature of certain

types of sports "instigate" eating disorders. Many studies have

proven these sports provoke prone athletes toward disordered

eating and exercising behaviors.

Although limited, eating disorder research with a male

sample of athletes often measure selected sports with the

highest known occurrences of anoxia or bulimia. This genre of

research centers upon three sport categories: 1) Appearance-

Based (e.g., diving, swimming), 2) Lean-Based (e.g., track, cross-

country), and 3) Weight-Restrictive (e.g., wresting, crew).

Within these particular sports, disorder eating is

considered "instrumental" or "functional" (Soutjesdyk & Jevne,

1993). Again, most of these studies exclude the EDNOS category even though the criterion remains most favorable for a male diagnosis. Although this narrow approach is exclusionary, it is within this section that the majority of male sport-related research on eating disorders has been done.

Appearance-Based. In sports judged by technical or artistic merit, there is an enormous pressure on the athlete to remain lean, as judges consider an aesthetic physique as a factor in scoring. Within these particular sports (e.g., gymnastics, diving), it is difficult to convince ill athletes of a need for treatment as body shape is a valid factor of judging. Theorists argue that this pressure to conform to an ideal sport-specific body type is aggravated by the revealing uniforms of these sports. This culture may increase the athlete's bodily self-awareness as their stature is evaluated and scored. As this culture is advanced inside of a team, the pressure of self-presentation is also increased.

Sports that require athletes to wear revealing clothing (swimming, track, volleyball) sends athletes a message that drives their need to be thinner to "look good" in their uniforms

(Cruse, 2003). Eating disorders can result as athletes participate in competitive thinness (group-think). This drive is propelled as athletes must wear a revealing uniform. Consequently, the athlete may compare their appearance to teammates (Cruse, 2003).

Outside of the environment of athletics, Fredrickson, Roberts, Noll, Quinn, and Twenge (1998) discerned parallels of females in revealing clothing severely increased body shame and restrictive eating. Feelings of shame and the act of restrictive eating increased further when before an audience. Along this line of conceptual thought, Reel and Gill (1996) confirmed the degree of revealing uniforms in cheerleading was a direct parallel to unhealthy behaviors to maintain a low body weight. The correlation between body dissatisfaction and eating disorders was also proven by the following scholars: Dummer, Rosen, Heusner, Roberts, and Cousilman, 1987; O'Connor, Lewis, and Kirchner, 1995; Petrie, 1993; and Ziegler and San-Khoo, 1998.

However, not all studies on uniform type yield clear

results of an inclination to eating disordered behaviors. By

comparing the emotional attitudes of athletes in different

uniforms, Krane, Waldron, Stiles-Shipley, and Michalenok (2001)

found perfectionism to be a factor of body dissatisfaction. This

is consistent with Brownell, Rodin, and Wilmore's 1992

observation that athletes have high levels of perfectionism that

lead to higher occurrences of anorexia and bulimia. In a similar

study to Krane, Waldron, Stiles-Shipley, and Michalenok (2001),

Fulkerson, Keel, Leon, and Dorr (1997) remarked that an athlete

with high levels of perfectionism also held a tendency for a

"drive for thinness" – an eating disorder criterion. Although

Krane, Waldron, Stiles-Shipley, and Michalenok's hypothesis of

elevated "social physique anxiety" among athletes with

revealing uniforms was not proven, they offered the

justification that collegiate athletes are accustomed to

competing in their sport's given uniform. Although both groups

sampled in the study (athletes and exercisers) had elevated

levels of anxiety of self-presentation, Krane mentioned the

sample of athlete may have developed coping skills in their many years of donning a revealing uniform.

Lean-Based. With a different theoretical premise than appearance-based sports, a perceived requirement of leanness to enhance athletic performance is believed to cause elevated rates of eating disorders in this category of sports. This drive to succeed can very easily become combined with the pressure to obtain the sport's idealist body type. If this occurs, an athlete predisposed to eating disorders may commit to a degree of eating and exercising confinement that will intensify the underlying cycle of control.

The drive to be lean is uniquely complex as it is manifested in America's unrealistic societal expectations. For athletes, a lifetime of manufactured images combined with the pressure to excel breeds a strong will to minimize levels of body fat. Student-athletes are frequently introduced to pathogenic methods of weight control by teammates and coaches (Stoutjesdyk & Jevne, 1993). A study conducted by Carter (2002), found 17.5% of college athletes who participated in

Division I lean-type sports exhibited eating disorder symptoms as only 9.2% of athletes in non-lean sports (e.g., basketball, football, hockey) displayed similar results. This statistic reveals the inherent risks of lean-type sports. In sports that lower body fat enhances performance (e.g., cross-country, gymnastics) very high rates of anorexia and bulimia are found. These types of sports that demand a thin physique and low weight or body fat have been shown to have higher a prevalence of eating disorders. The widespread belief by athletes and coaches that extra weight diminishes performance by decreasing speed, endurance and agility is a clear factor that leads to disordered eating behaviors in this category of sports. Addressing this belief, Bruch (1981) asserted in his research findings that those with disordered eating behaviors are a perceived response to peripheral demands, not personal wants.

Weight-Restricted. The most visible sport that eating disorder behaviors can be observed as normative behaviors is the preparation of competitive wrestlers. The 1997 deaths of three intercollegiate wrestlers prompted the NCAA and associated governing bodies to establish policies that prohibit and regulate the common and unsafe weight loss practices of college wrestlers. New regulations include an adjustment to all weight categories, a weight class certification process and decreased time between weigh-ins and competition. The later change serves to avoid binge eating after several days of food restriction. The policy also discourages wrestlers from losing too much weight as the policy does not allow adequate time to re-feed and re-hydrate to increase strength before their match. Furthermore, traditional dehydration practices were outlawed, such common forms of purging include: the use of vapor-impermeable suits, saunas, and excessive cardiovascular exercise.

Even with these new regulations, unhealthy behaviors are still prevalent among wrestlers, such as laxative and water pill abuses. It is common for college wrestlers to engage in rapid weight loss (RWL) techniques (Dick, Oppliger, Scott, & Utter, 1992). These methods affect the student-athlete's physical and mental health. Engaging the RWL techniques can cause death from the extreme nature of the methods. Adding to the risk, collegiate wrestlers must "make weight" several times during a season, 15-20 times is common. This dramatic decrease and increase of body weight places severe stress on the wrestler's body and mind. For decades, competitive wrestlers have relied on RWL with the purpose of qualifying for a specific weight class. In a 1992 observation by the NCAA, it was discovered that the majority of competitors employed severe weight loss techniques prior to the 1992 NCAA Championships, losing an average of eight pounds within days prior to their competition (Dick, Oppliger, Scott, & Utter, 1992).

Since the onset of the NCAA's interception of historically dangerous weight-loss practices, several studies found a decline of RWL practices in wrestling – none more convincing then the Scott et al's study of the NCAA's new rule change by comparing the average weight loss of wrestlers in the 1999 NCAA Championship. With new regulations in place, wresters lost an average of only a pound and a half as compared to the eight pounds at 1992 Championship. Scott et al's research (among others) confirmed that effectiveness of the NCAA's actions in the formation of new policies.

However, Alderman, Carlson, Landers, and Scott's 2003 study also focused on rapid weight loss practices of college wrestlers, a population not exempt from the reach of the NCAA's 1992 policy. Alderman's research provided a glimpse into the practices of collegiate wrestlers and the effectiveness of enforcing the NCAA's policies on an institutional level. Alderman found rapid weight loss techniques to be commonplace among the international wrestling population. Popular techniques (all types of purging) included excessive running, cycling, swimming, sauna, and steam room use, and plastic warm-up suits. Further forms of purging consisted of excessive vomiting, and the use of diuretics and laxatives. From RWL techniques, Alderman's sample population admitted to experiencing headaches (47%), severe dizziness (44%), hot flashes (22%), nausea (42%), nose bleeds (20%), feverish (18%), disorientation (9%), and racing heart rates (4%).

Notably, Alderman found higher placed wrestlers had more dramatic weight loss-gain. Within his sample of 2,638 wrestlers, the highest weight loss before a competition was 22.55-pounds, with an 11-pound average. The mean weight gain after the season was 10.7-pounds. On average, wrestlers in the 154 to 164-pound weight class loss the most weigh. Junior wrestlers had the most dramatic weight loss-gains, followed by freshmen. Even with risking disqualification for violating the NCAA's policy, Alderman reported a 40 to 60% RWL abuse.

Reinforcing the group-think culture within wrestling, both athletes and coaches tend to justify RWL practices as it benefits performance by bettering leverage and strength over smaller opponents. Despite studies proving physiological and psychological disturbances, RWL practices are commonplace as this sport culture produces high diagnoses of bulimia. The most disturbing aspect of Alderman's study is the encouragement of these practices by coaches. It is reports such as these that add a significant and overwhelming amount of pressure on a student-athlete to conform.

The EDBT Category and Males

"If male athletes feel they are not lean and muscular enough and combined that with unhealthy eating behaviors it could result in a body image disorder known as muscle dysmorphia [a category identical in nature to EDBT]*"* (Carter, 2002).

While regarded as health enhancing, exercise has also been acknowledged as having the potential to be a harmful obsession (Morgan & Russell, 1975). A fixation on exercise can lead to symptoms of withdrawal upon discontinuation, disturbed progression of clear thoughts, and the interference with social relationships and professional obligations (Morgan & Russell, 1975). Through advanced research on unhealthy exercise patterns, this obsession has gained the attention of the medical field.

According to studies by Anderson, Basson and Geils (1997), Thornton and Scott (1995), and Pierce, Daleng, and McGowen (1993), eating disorders and excessive exercising occur in tandem. Perhaps, as some researchers have suggested, *"exercise dependence may be largely an expression of an underlying eating disorder"* (Bamber, Cockerill, Rogers, &

Carroll, 2000). In his 1995 study, Veale recognized this link, and was first to introduce the term "secondary exercise dependence" to clarify self-imposed obligatory exercise as an aspect of eating disorders. Recently, authors have coined this breed of athletes with different terms that define the same condition: "anorexia athletica," "muscle dysmorphia," "reverse anorexia," "secondary anorexia," "exercise anorexia," and the most recent term of "manorexia."

Harvard University Medical School researchers Amanda Gruber and Harrison Pope developed the provisional medical diagnostic criteria for this disorder in their 2000 study entitled *Psychiatric and Medical Effects of Anabolic-Androgenic Steroid Use in Women*. In the process of sampling female competitive bodybuilders and dedicated weight-lifters, Gruber and Pope found a striking commonality of adverse eating habits that although very abnormal, did not met any of the DSM-IV's eating disorders criteria. In their study's findings, Gruber and Pope (2000) offered proposed criteria for the condition they termed "Eating Disorder Bodybuilding Type" or EDBT since the sport of competitive bodybuilding normative behaviors relies so heavily

on these types of disorder eating behaviors and beliefs. Gruber

and Pope (2000) described EDBT as a preoccupation and strict

adherence to a specific diet that is consumed in the form of pre-

prepared meals and supplements eaten at regularly scheduled

intervals.

These Harvard researchers found people with EDBT

often refuse to eat at restaurants or friends houses because of

their obsessive need to be certain that they were ingesting the

precise amounts of calories, protein, fat, and carbohydrates

believed essential to maintain their physique. Gruber and

Pope's (2000) criteria may be considered to be added as sub-

clinical eating disorder with the release of the DSM-V in 2011.

In a 2001 study, Mangweth et al. compared the

perceived body images, psychopathology, and sexual histories

of college male bodybuilders, college men with eating disorders,

and normalized eating males. The sample consisted of twenty-

eight male bodybuilders and thirty-three men with normalized

eating, and thirty men with eating disorders (anorexia nervosa, bulimia or binge eating disorder as defined by DSM-IV). The study found the bodybuilders exhibited a pattern of eating and exercising just as obsessive as those with eating disorders. However, the bodybuilders had a reverse focus of gaining muscle as opposed to losing fat. Bodybuilders and men with eating disorders scored similarly in their history of psychiatric disorders. In measures of body image, the bodybuilder sample also closely resembled the men with eating disorders. Only a lack of sexual desire was reported more often by both bodybuilders and men with eating disorders. Mangweth et al. concluded that bodybuilders share many features (eating behaviors and body image) of individuals with eating disorders.

By the nature of their chosen environment, athletes pursue the unremitting goal of optimal performance. This drive for success can develop into a perpetual cycle of striving to obtain an illusive and idealist goal. With hope of attainment, this may lead to unhealthy obsessions with exercise and food. Athletes with high degrees of perfection and obsession tend to befit easily into this newly recognized disorder.

With the requisite personality traits, athletes experiencing situations that threaten their self-imposed rigid training and eating schedules will encounter high levels of anxiety from their lack of control. The athlete's anxiety will increase with the uncertainty of when and where the individual will eat; how much body weight believed they will incur in a meal with friends / family; enduring rumination of thoughts of how they can avoid eating "banned" foods in social situations; and of the amount of added exercise they must endure to counter an unplanned meal or the consumption of forbidden food.

In most cases, disordered eating and exercising athletes began with standard diet or exercise regimen. Oddly, predisposed athletes are driven to self-impose a more stringent diet and exercise routine as an underlying form of self-punishment. In doing so, what began as a healthy fitness program is transformed into compulsivity and adherence to a self-imposed rigid exercise and dietary regimen in a concentrated, narrow drive to obtain an illusive goal.

Research on EDBT

"Exercise dependence [the primary indicator of EDBT] *may be largely an expression of an underlying eating disorder"* (Bamber, Cockerill, Rogers, & Carroll, 2000).

The section to follow is a synthesis of the history and research on this new category, from it's inception as "subclinical anorexia," evolving to the popular term of "muscle dysmorphia" and "anorexia athletica," and the Gruber and Pope (2000) classification of "EDBT." Upon further study of this disorder, many experts anticipate a societal change of eating disorder perceptions as EDBT criteria addresses fixations on body image and shape with ill-perception of muscularity that primarily affects males. The behaviors that lead to the specific criteria for this disorder are similar in their pathogenic and maladaptive context to anorexia and bulimia, yet they are more accepting to ill males with athletic fixations.

As research on this new classification began to surface, Norwegian eating disorders expert, Sundgot-Borgen (1994a), initially termed this athletic obsession as "sub-clinical anorexia."

Her early description of the disorder was a strongly committed athlete that underwent self-imposed extreme means to improve the chance of succeeding in their sport (Sundgot-Borgen, 1994a). Yet, with the consuming control of an eating disorder, dieting and maintenance for a provisional body type becomes "no longer the means to an end as athletic success became the end in itself" (Smith, et al., 1998, p. 139). As further scholarship emerged, Sundgot-Borgen (1994a) developed specific criteria her newly termed condition of "anorexia athletica." However, Arizona State University researchers opposed and disputed the criteria, claiming her standards were "ill-defined and indiscriminate" (Beals and Manore, 1994, p. 175). As a result, new studies emerged in an attempt to better understand, thus define, this condition.

Although most research on the drive for thinness is centered on females, studies that have surveyed males produced significant results. The standard of attractiveness for the male physique has evolved to bigger and more muscular. McCreary, Sasse, and Doris (2000) claimed males are drawn to muscularity in the same way females are motivated to be thin.

The underpinning physiological motivator for both genders is

identical - poor self-esteem and high levels of depression.

McCreary and Sasse's research acknowledged a shared drive for

thinness between females and male athletes. Their research

also revealed that males often aspire to attain a muscular

mesomorphic physique, as males tend to be of the opinion that

females prefer this appearance. This assumption has been

validated by many empirical studies, discovering females do

prefer the classic inverted triangular physique of males.

Popular western culture continuously reinforces the

association between male muscularity and masculinity. This

prevalent cultural norm depicts the ideal male build as a lean,

toned mesomorphic shape. Yet males most often do not labor

to obtain this physique for its health benefits. Rather, males will

endure strenuous workouts and strict diets to obtain a physique

that symbolizes control, masculinity, self-discipline,

competence, and sexual desirability (Raphael & Lacey, 1992;

Striegel-Moore, Silberstein, & Rodin, 1986).

Symptomatic of eating disorder etiology, research on the male's drive for muscularity found between 28 and 68% of normal weight males trying to gain weight to pacify their distorted body image, seeing themselves as "thinner and less muscular than they really are" (McCreary, Sasse, & Doris, 2000, p. 298). This condition is known as body dysmorphia or having a distorted body image. A 1997 study at the University of Pennsylvania supported McCreary, Sasse, and Doris' 2000 findings as their sample consistently selected an illustrated physique that most closely identified their own from a range of silhouettes. Both genders tended to select images larger then their physiques. Noting the influence of Western culture on males, the sample of males frequently selected an enlarge size as their ideal.

Derived from Bruch's 1979 research findings on fear of obesity and the distortion of body image, contributing author of *Exacting Beauty: Theory, Assessment, and Treatment of Body Image Disturbances* (1999), J. Kevin Thompson claims body image is an internal view of one's appearance, commenting:

The primary feature is a person's extreme

disparagement of some aspect of his / her

appearance. Importantly, rating of the body

feature does not fit with that of an objective

observer. What perhaps is most important from

a clinical viewpoint is that the individual is

obsessively focused with that person's

existence (p. 11).

In a qualitative study by Bamber, Cockerill, Rodgers, and Carroll

(2000), eight female subjects were screened for exercise

dependence and eating disorders. The researchers inquired

about the sample's history of psychological distress and their

eating and exercise behaviors. The study found *exercise*

dependence always manifested with those diagnosed with an

eating disorder. Initiating research on the use of anabolic-

androgenic steroids in women, Gruber and Pope (2000)

performed psychiatric and medical evaluations of 75 dedicated

women athletes. The researchers found twenty-five subjects (30

and 33%) were current or past steroid users. Perhaps the most interesting and relevant findings to this review was the

identification of several unusual psychiatric syndromes reported

by both the steroid users and nonusers. These rigid dietary

practices were measured using Gruber and Pope's EDBT criteria.

This finding was unexpected, but resulted from the usually high

occurrences of chronic dissatisfaction and preoccupation with

their physiques (EDBT).

In 2002, Blaydon, Lindner, and Kerr hypothesized that

an eating disorder or exercise dependence is the motivation to

train for competitive athletes. In the study's sample, 171 tri-

athletes were measuring for eating disorders and exercise

dependence by utilizing separate assessment instruments. The

athletes that met the DSM-IV's standards for eating disorders

held significant tendencies of exercise dependency.

Furthermore, this group was more apt to obtain a set goal,

master their sport and enjoy the status they received.

Thompson's 1999 book investigated body dysmorphia

as it relates to EDBT's eating disorder symptomology: excessive

dieting, weight loss / gain, purging, and feelings of lost control around food. In regards to distorted body images, Thompson (1999) observed that most often the eating disordered person's perception is not distorted, rather, it is more likely that their view of their appearance is "disliked, disparaged, or seen as unacceptable" (p. 11). This feature of eating disorders contributes to the mental confusion caused by the disease. Poor body image will often lead to higher levels of self-consciousness and social avoidance (Thompson, 1999). The body image is considered "disturbed" when it interferes with social or professional functioning or causes a high level of anxiety or depression (Thompson, 1999). Thompson, an eating disorder expert at the University of South Florida, affirms findings that suggest body image dysmorphia is highly present in those with EDNOS and EDBT diagnoses and less so among the anorexia or bulimia populations.

A study of 882 student-athletes at Ohio State University by Carter in 2002 on muscle dysmorphia identified the female athlete population desired an average weight loss of 6.8 pounds. Conversely, men favored an average weight gain of 3.2

pounds. Carter found 1.1% of Ohio State's male athletes supported the diagnosis. Carter's examination on student-athlete's body image revealed 9% abused performance-enhancing drugs or supplements; 5% avoided situations in exposing their bodies; 4% were preoccupied with a perceived inadequacy of their body size; and 4% admitted to forgoing academic or social activities for exercise sessions or diet schedule. Through studying the results of his sample, Carter claimed at the 2002 the annual meeting of the American Psychological Association, "If male athletes feel they are not lean and muscular enough – and combined that with unhealthy eating behaviors – it could result in a body image disorder known as muscle dysmorphia."

Research on this topic has begun to establish males as more motivated to engage in weight training and increased sessions as a direct correlation to their body satisfaction, regardless of their muscle mass (Rosen & Gross, 1987; Cohn, 2000; Drewnowski & Yee, 1987; Hueneman, Mahamedi, Stripe, & Field, 1997; Kelly, Pattern & Johannes, 1982; Raudenbush &

Zellner, 1997; and Wang, et al. 1994). A 2004 article by

McCreary, Sasse, Saucier, and Dorsch suggested the

psychological process of excess in either gender's motivation to

be thin or muscular is internalized in the same way. Just as

those with a "drive for thinness" will abuse laxatives, adhere to

strict diet regimens, and practice self-induced vomiting,

individuals with a "drive for muscularity" will engage in binge

eating without purging and excessive exercise. This account is

consistent with the NCAA's 1991 study that identified male

athletes as most likely to engage in binge eating as compared to

their female counterparts. Consequently, the psychological

consequences of EDBT do not differ in severity from an affliction

of anorexia or bulimia.

Among athletes with either of the four (including EDBT)

eating disorders, control and rigorous, restrictive dieting is a

shared aspect. In addition to those forms of purging, many

athletes will also engage in a purging routine that consists of

laxative and diuretic abuse, self-induced vomiting, and most commonly, excessive exercise. Compulsive exercise is often central to an athlete's eating disorder.

The message in Figure 7 is a common belief promoted in advertisements that target males in fitness magazines. Most advertisements of this nature seek to validate their product through unnatural muscular images of the male physique, and often refer to excesses in eating or exercising as a means to prove masculinity. One educated in eating disorders would consider the below advertisement as an endorsement for disordered eating and exercising behaviors to reach a high degree of muscularity and masculinity.

A recent report by the Renfrew Center stated 28% of high school male's sole reason for weight lifting was in an attempt to gain weight. Early reports on the new classification estimate that 2% of Americans have EDBT. This condition is identified by a lack of control over excessive appearance concerns, perceived lack of muscle, distorted body image, and distress in social or occupational environments. Researchers from Arizona State University have petitioned for a clear definition of EDBT. Without a criteria set this classification will be subjectively defined. The forthcoming DSM-V may add the classification of EDBT as a eating disorder category whose criteria will encompass the research on the topic, regardless of past terminology or criteria.

Most of the research on this subject can be summarized in the article, *It's Exercise or Nothing* (Bamber, et al. 2000). The researchers conducted a qualitative analysis of exercise dependency with striking findings as the portion of the sample labeled as "exercise dependant" all displayed the criteria for anorexia, bulimia, and EDNOS. Additionally, those addicted to their control over exercise reported high levels of psychological distress - a shared aspect that indicates the progression of eating disorders.

Impact on Higher Education

"Bulimia first came to widespread public notoriety in the United States through a spate of articles in the popular press, including an article in the New York Times describing a study that had documented a virtual epidemic on a campus of the State University of New York" (Gordon, 2000, p. 3).

Empirical studies with college populations have greatly enhanced eating disorder etiology. In particular, this research has increased the field's degree of understanding into the differential risk factors of specific college groups. Within this review of eating disorder literature, the majority of citations are from studies that sampled a college population. The college environment of discovery and personal growth is unique in its ability to allow its members to "rediscover" themselves and form a new identify. Yet this process occurs among varying degrees of readiness, as one's comfort in releasing control in order to grow is often tested. Research on the college student has established higher clinical and sub-clinical eating disorder prevalence rates among the traditional college student. This is particularly true for students participating in varsity athletics,

transitioning to their freshman year, recognize their sexual

identity, searching for self-identification within a group; and

attempting to maintain a high academic, athletic, or social

status (Crowther, Wolf, & Sherwood, 1992; Fairburn & Cooper,

1993; Gordon, 1990; Hoek, 1995; Shisslak, Crago, & Estes,

1995).

The growing number of college students exhibiting

disordered eating behaviors impacts higher education in several

ways. Case studies show it is practically impossible to maintain

an eating disorder without compromising one's social life,

health or academic function. Given the high presence of

disordered eating behaviors within a college and collegiate

athletics, institutions must engage in an approach that is

preventative as well as intervening. Among many reports on

prevalence of eating disorder behaviors in college, one study

reported that up to 62% of college women routinely displayed

pathogenic weight control behaviors (Dummer, Rosen, Heusner,

Roberts, & Cousilman, 1987). Studies that examined the

female's experience on transitioning from high school to college estimate a substantial increased in risk between four and 19%

(Borgen & Corbin, 1987).

This finding suggests the transition into higher

education in itself is a risk factor. Kirk, Singh, and Getz (2002)

predicted this increased risk originates from the "lack of

predictability in the new environment, different social codes of

conduct, higher demands for academic performance, and little

or no access to adult guidance" (p. 123). A similar study by

Skowron & Friedlander (1994) hypothesized a difficult college

transition can cause students to pursue extreme athletic

measures to distinguish themselves among their peers and

parents.

The article, *More Than Just Food: Students Suffer from

the Challenges of Eating Disorders* (Bergeron, 2004), addressed

the aspects of a college environment that are present to cause a

higher risk of eating disorders. In the American culture,

attending college is perceived as a "right of passage" to

independence and adulthood. This new autonomy, friendships,

and pressures may create unanticipated stress. A study in the

Journal of Counseling Psychology reported that eating disorders
are relatively common on college campuses, as upwards of 15%
of undergraduate women have significant disordered eating
attitudes and behaviors.

According to Becker, Keel, Anderson-Fye, Thomas
(2004), the presence of eating disorders among college-aged
females positioned this population to be at serious
psychological and medical risk. With this, efforts to develop
effective means of preventing and treating eating disorders are
limited by the incomplete understanding of the disease's
multifactorial etiology. Whereas epidemiologic data suggests a
strong socio-cultural influence to moderate the risk, many
theorists speculate on their influence, as the aspect has
remained empirically unevaluated. Observational information
suggests that social transitions, Western media exposure, and
specific peer environments (social comparison and teasing)
contribute to an increased risk.

A study by Root, Fallon, and Friedrich (1987)
determined that unprepared adolescents confronted with new

situations often display anorexic behaviors to cope with feelings

of uncertainty. Further validating the inherent risk of a high

school to college transition, studies have concluded that older

college students are far less likely to develop an eating disorder.

In Heatherton, Mahamedi, Stripe, and Field (1997), their

research findings proved increased age is a protective factor

from eating disorders among college students. The

developmental aspects of protection found were self-

maturation, exposure to new ideas, and a better sense of self.

The college environment has been referred to as a

"breeding ground" for eating disorders (Sparks, 2005). The

collective internal and external aspects of a college culture

increase the risk for those that inhabit this environment.

Although the length of illness is very much dependent on the

time of detection and quality of treatment, the common ages of

onset have been determined. Eating disorders most frequently

develop during adolescence and early adulthood – the same age

range for 45.2% of all American undergraduate students (ages

fifteen to twenty-one). Ninety percent of women with eating

disorders are between the ages of twelve and twenty-five with

a median age of seventeen and a mean age of eighteen

(Renfrew Center Foundation, Nattiv, Agostini & Drinkwater,

1994). Statistics confirm a mean female diagnosis age for

anorexia is between 13 and 20. A later age for the same

diagnosis is 18 for males. The delay is from the difficulties in

identifying the illness in males. The later statistic is disturbing

considering the mean onset age for males is 13.7. This suggests

males suffer and worsen for a four-year average before they are

even diagnosed, let alone enter treatment. The average onset

age for bulimia is later than anorexia. The reported age range

for females with bulimia is 16 to 18 and 18 to 26 for males.

Consequently, males can have the same bulimic symptoms as

females for an estimated ten years prior to a medical diagnosis.

   With almost half of all college students falling within the

age range for anorexia and bulimia, American higher education

is faced with an unwavering fact that a significant portion of

their populace engages in varying degrees of pathogenic and

maladaptive eating disordered behaviors. In a survey of 226

college students, 44% of females and 24% of males were attempting to lose weight – females primarily used dietary restrictions as males abused exercise (Drewnoski & Yee, 1987). With the mounting of similar data, eating disorder behaviors are an inherent problem for this nation's 4,048 colleges and universities with the expectation to expand. The percentage of college students between the ages of 18-24 has grown substantially, from 30.9% in 1989 to 43.8% in 1999. Within six years an additional 243,000 students between the ages of 18 and 19 will be enrolled in an American college or university (Chronicle of Higher Education, Almanac Edition, 2001). With an expected increased in enrollment, American institutions must be equipped to address the spike of psychological and physiological issues that will infect a campus.

A 2002 study by Prouty, Protinsky, and Canady found 17% of college students meet anorexia or bulimia criteria. This figure was substantiated further by Ross and Gill's 2002 study that identified up to 20% of all college women report symptoms of eating disorders. The research Prouty, Protinsky, and Canady

(2002) concluded that the majority of ill students were white,

female, in a sorority, and of a Christian-based faith. The authors

purposed an increase in eating disorder awareness on American

campuses. This recommendation stemmed from a disturbing

and unexpected research finding that the majority of student's

symptoms worsened because treatment was not sought in the

early stages of the disease. The major finding of the study was

identifying the tendency for college student to confide in a

friend prior to seeking a medical intervention. Prouty, Protinsky,

and Canady's 2002 study reinforced the importance of regularly

assessing the presence of eating disorders on a college campus.

This will help prepare an institution's medical staff for the

possible up flow of ill late adolescent and young adult students.

As ill students seek advice from peers before a college mental

health professional is involved, the authors recommended

integrating campus teams to increase the interaction of

administrators with students (Prouty, Protinsky, & Canady,

2002).

Research by Monteath and McCabe (1997) revealed a high degree of eating disordered attitudes among college women. In this study, 56% of the respondents felt pressure to maintain a particular bodyweight. This pressure was reported to most often originate from mothers. Boyfriends were cited as the second highest source of pressure, followed by peers. The author's results substantiated other study's findings on dissatisfied body weight among college students as Monteath and McCabe's sample desired a much lower weight than their actual. More than a third preferred a ten to nineteen pound weight-loss. One in ten sought to loss twenty or more pounds. Fifty-nine percent of the sample had dieted an average of four times during the past year. These results are supported by an earlier study: Schulken, Pinciaro, Sawyer, Jenson, and Hoban (1997). While the implications for this study are coupled with unrealistic body weight expectations, the high rate of dieting is a risk factor because of the inherent negative attitudes toward one's body image (Story et al., 1991).

Quantifying a common eating disorder behavior within higher education, a 2004 exploratory study from Garman, Hayduck, Crider, and Hodel researched and publicized the most prevalent negative health behaviors in American colleges and universities. By conducting their own study and including the mean results of twenty-five related studies, the researchers established compulsive exercising as a prominent behavior among college students.

According to James Rippe of Tufts University, compulsive and obsessive exercise is a common form of purging that incorporates a drive for thinness, obligatory behaviors, and the pacification of an intense fear of gaining body fat. Moreover, Rippe claims *colleges and universities can be an addictive "breeding grounds of eating disorders"* [emphasis mine.] As a leading eating disorder behavior, indicator, and symptom, compulsive exercise is ranked fourth among mean occurrences of unhealthy college behaviors, only slightly behind marijuana use (Figure 9).

Eating disorders are one of the major health issues facing American teenagers and young adults. Studies conducted in the last decade show that eating disorders and disordered eating behaviors are related to other health risk behaviors, including tobacco use, alcohol use, marijuana use, delinquency, unprotected sexual activity, and suicide attempts. With this, unhealthy behaviors common in higher education may stem from the substantial number of students with eating disorders of disorder eating behaviors. This parallel is an added concern for higher education as students with eating disorders are increasing (Granner, Abood, & Black, 2001).

According to Arnold Anderson, co-author of *Making Weight* (2000), Director of John Hopkins' Eating Disorder Program, and professor of psychiatry at the University of Iowa, the reported number of males with eating disorders has grown. Anderson estimated 25% of those with a diagnosable eating disorder are male. Graham reported that an estimated 150,000 (mostly undetected) college men have an eating disorder (Graham, 2004). This is congruent with eating disorder expert,

Ron Thompson's belief that "Athletes are more at risk for eating disorders than non-athletes, but they are also under-identified," (Cruse, 2003). Based on the related studies in this review, Anderson's estimate may fall at the lower end of his projected figure.

Even with new empirical data on the increasing presence of males with eating disorders, the illness remains stereotyped as a "female disease." On many American campuses, there is a commonality of gender-specific programming and awareness-building events specific to the female population. As colleges and universities adopt national campaigns (e.g., Eating Disorder Awareness Week) many institutions give their events a female-specific name, theme, and focus. The state of Utah's 2001 campaign was incorporated into many of the state higher education health and wellness programming. Yet, the female slant of the theme certainly excluded males and promoted existing stereotypes: "Help Put the Light Back in *Her* [emphasis mine] Eyes". With years of shunning the male population, new information has emerged on the undetected degree of males with eating disorders. As a result, a conscious emphasis in research and promotion needs to be given to male body image concerns.

A Princeton University study found 150,000 men in American colleges have an eating disorder (Graham, 2004). As a result, Princeton developed a task force in 2002 that reported the number of male and female college students with eating disorders is "apparently large and growing." Consequently, the task force implemented a weekly support group exclusive to male Princeton students and recommended further researcher on college males to aide in higher education retention,

> Unless they seek treatment, men with eating disorders do not fare well in college. If fact, their problem [eating disorder] can get worse, as stressors of life, work, relationships and the real world lead them to use food – or a lack of it – as a coping strategy (Graham, 2004 in *College Men Increasingly Suffer from Eating Disorders, Partly Pressured by Athletics*.)

Harvard Medical School's Roberto Olivardia co-authored the book, *The Adonis Complex: The Secret Crisis of Male Body Obsession* and reported that Ivy League schools experience higher occurrences of male eating disorders. Olivardia cites the connection between college and disordered eating is strong, "While it is unclear exactly how many men develop eating disorders in college, we know that eating disorders tend to affect college men versus men who do not attend college" (Graham, 2004).

Aside from anorexia and bulimia, a new front of eating disorders is emerging into eating disorder research. The EDNOS category is severely understudied, yet when controlled for unparallel results are yielded. The pending eating disorder category, EDBT, is also gaining in popularity among literature and research. McCreary, Sasse, and Doris (2000) examined the prevalence and practices in the college student's drive for muscularity. As women are most likely to adopt an obsessive lifestyle in their drive for thinness, men are equally as likely to engage in mirrored behaviors in a quest to be muscular.

When exploring the disparity of eating attitudes and behaviors among genders, Nelson et al. (1999) found similar gender symptoms as both sexes exhibited high rates of psychological distress and negative self-concepts. Although the study confirmed a similarity of eating disorder symptomology, the researchers did conclude that their high unexpected detection of males with the disease suggest, "eating disorders may be more prevalent among males than previously estimated" (Nelson et al., p. 7). A similar conclusion was found in Nelson, et al.'s 2004 study. As the study did not sample a traditionally high scoring population, the authors were "particularly disturbed" from the unexpected high prevalence of eating disordered males.

The findings of high prevalence rates in EDNOS research and in the forthcoming eating disorder classification, EDBT, will affect higher education on many fronts. Higher education counselors, medical staff, and athletic coaches are familiar in detecting eating disorders in women. As early diagnosis is paramount to recovery, many indicators are revealed in high school athletics. Unfortunately, beyond significant weight loss,

most high school administrators are unfamiliar with the

common emotional and physical eating disorder symptoms.

With 18 and 21 as the respective mean ages of onset for

female and males, the onus of detection, awareness, education,

and prevention befalls on higher education. It is college culture

that research has suggested to be the collective environment

that initiates eating disorder pathology (Person, Benson-

Quaziena, & Rogers, 2001). As eating disorders originate and

primarily affect one's psychological rational, recovery is

obtained through early detection and counseling - an aspect of

in loco parentis (Latin for "in the place of a parent") inherent to

the conscientious American college and university.

Summary

While eating disorders are an assumed female affliction,

the disease's presence in males has grown to an undetermined

level. Considering the standard estimate that males account for

10% of all American eating disorder cases, hundreds of

thousands of men are ill in an environment that does not recognize their illness. Consequently, this conservative estimate still renders eating disorders as a significant health issue for males. Yet, estimates cannot account for the portion of males that are commonly unidentified or misdiagnosed.

This truth is disheartening when considering occurrences of eating disorders are at their highest in college. Unfortunately, this environment does not differ from others in the difficulty of recognizing eating disorders in male students. Even among physicians, this flawed ability to detect is in part a result of the popular opinion that eating disorders are a female disease.

However, there are indications that this belief is changing. The growth of America's fitness culture has modernized the "ideal" male physique, causing a deepened distress for men and their body image. This concern is particularly rampant in the culture of male college athletics as physique and success is linked to the athlete's degree of masculinity. To advance the etiology of male eating disorders, further scholarship is needed on the flawed relationship with food and exercise to define the need for success in the realm of sports.

Understanding the deficiencies within eating disorder literature, this research is designed to study aspects of eating disorders that had promising, but understudied results. With this direction, the study will be an inclusive representation of disordered eating behaviors within the most common varsity sports that college males inhabit. To position this study away from the masses of existing research and their biases, the study will have a direct focus to explore: 1) The presence of the EDNOS, disordered eating, and the EDBT categories; 2) An exclusive male sample; and 3) A range of varsity sports.

This approach is unlike the majority of research that often centers on a female sample with anorexia and bulimia in selected sports with a proven history of elevated disease occurrences. While these routinely examined sports will be included, other collegiate sports (such as football) that are often excluded from eating disordered research will be represented.

Decades of studies that excluded males have led to a cavity in scholarly literature. In so doing, myths and stereotypes were formed and augmented. Thus, they became so ingrained in our culture that they biased and hindered clinical judgments, medical diagnoses, and treatment plans. Theoretically, further study on males can only contribute to eating disorder etiology and promote the true aspects of the disease. Advancement in this area will lead to a greater understanding of eating disorders. Furthermore, a more truthful account of ill males may be obtained by reducing the disease's stigma by increased societal awareness that the disease as affects and is equally severe to both genders. As a result, suffering males may come forth and physicians may hold a higher tolerance of the disease's gender neutrality. If forthcoming studies continue to agree with the gender commonalities of predisposing traits, than the sociological stigmatic view of males with eating disorders may lose credibility (Carlat, Camargo, & Herzog, 1997).

CHAPTER THREE: METHODOLOGY

Introduction

In response to the conceptual and theoretical views and the related literature on eating disorder etiology and the common research practices discussed in Chapters One and Two, this third chapter outlines the methodology of this study. This exploratory, quantitative study was approved by the University of Buffalo's Social and Behavioral Sciences Institutional Review Board (SBSIRB) on January 3, 2007 (Study Number 2526). The study has three research questions:

1. Among male varsity student-athletes who compete in the Mid-American Conference, what is the presence of anorexia and bulimia as defined by the American Psychiatric Association (2004) and EDBT as determined by Gruber and Pope's 2000 research?

2. Among male varsity student-athletes who compete in the Mid-American Conference, will the EDNOS category be the most common clinical eating disorder by exceeding the sample's occurrences of anorexia and bulimia?

3. Among male varsity student-athletes who compete in the Mid-American Conference, will the sample's sport be correlated to the presence of anorexia, bulimia, EDNOS, or EDBT?

Subjects

Mid-American Conference Varsity Male Student-Athletes.

The subjects for this study are male student-athletes

who participate in a Mid-American Conference (MAC) varsity

sport during the 2006-2007 academic year (fall and spring

semesters). An eligible subject must be a full-time male student,

enrolled in a MAC institution, in good athletic standing as

determined by their institution, and a member of an exclusive

male varsity sport team. A varsity team is defined as the

principal team representing the institution in organized sport

competitions, as it is distinctly different in culture and

membership from a club or recreational team.

Mid-American Conference. The Mid-American

Conference (MAC) is a collegiate athletic league founded in

1946 and is based in Cleveland, Ohio with nearly 1.7 million

alumni nationwide. The MAC has two divisions, East and West,

and a membership of twelve institutions. These member

institutions are mainly located in the Midwestern United States

as nine of the twelve schools are in Ohio and Michigan. In 2006, the MAC ranked highest among all eleven NCAA Division I-AA

conferences in graduation rates. With an estimated student

population of 240,000 and an institution average of 22,000, the

Mid-American conference is the fourth largest Division I-A

conference in terms of undergraduate population and is the

third largest Division I-A conference in terms of total

enrollment. The following states are conference members:

Illinois (1); Indiana (1); Michigan (3); Ohio (6); and New York (1).

Appendages A and B provide a demographic overview

of the MAC institutions and student-athlete populations for the

2005-2006 academic year. This information was obtained per

the Equity in Athletics Disclosure Act (EADA). As yearly

participant numbers of individual college sport teams will only

vary slightly, the information in these two appendages is an

accurate reflection of this studies sample population.

MAC Institutions as a Survey Item. After a student-

athlete provides his informed consent, the responder is directed

to the survey's second page. As shown in Appendage D, this

page includes a drop-down listing of all MAC member

institutions. Student-athlete's can only select a single MAC institution. Although Western Michigan University declined to participate in this study, they were included in the list of schools so all MAC member institutions were represented. The twelve response options (i.e., MAC member institutions) for this survey item were: Ball State University, Bowling Green State University, Central Michigan University, Eastern Michigan University, Kent State University, Miami University, Northern Illinois University, Ohio University, University of Akron, University at Buffalo, University of Toledo, and Western Michigan University.

This data from this survey item was used to track each school's progress of their male student-athlete's responses. The absence or minimal responses from schools that agreed to facilitate the survey were sent additional requests via email and telephone. The data from this survey item will not be used to correlate the eating disorder presence of each school.

Operationalized Variables

Independent Variable (Operationalized)

Male Varsity Sport Team: The second page of the survey

(Appendage D) allows the student-athlete to select the varsity

sport or sports (up to two sports can be selected) that he is a

member. This data will allow for correlation of sport and eating

disorders prevalence. The survey response options are baseball,

basketball, combined track, football, golf, ice hockey, soccer,

swimming or diving, tennis, volleyball, and wrestling. These

eleven sports are exclusive male varsity sports that are common

among some or all of the MAC member institutions.

Dependent Variables (Operationalized)

Presence of Anorexia Nervosa: The three APA criteria for a male

diagnosis of anorexia are asked in survey questions #11-13

(Appendage F). As with all of the diagnostic criteria in the

survey, the Likert scale responses are paired and assigned

numerical values: "Always" and "Usually" (numerical value of

two), "Often" and "Sometimes" (numerical value of one),

"Rarely" or "Never" (numerical value of zero). For a student-athlete to be diagnosed with anorexia, he must confirm all three diagnostic criteria by self-reporting a response of "Always" or "Usually" and thereby receiving an overall numerical score of six for the three anorexia survey items.

Presence of Bulimia Nervosa: The four APA criteria for a diagnosis of bulimia are asked in survey questions #14-17 (Appendage G). The Likert scale responses are paired and assigned numerical values: "Always" and "Usually" (numerical value of two), "Often" and "Sometimes" (numerical value of one), "Rarely" or "Never" (numerical value of zero). For a student-athlete to be diagnosed with bulimia, they must confirm all four diagnostic criteria by self-reporting a response of "Always" or "Usually" thus receiving an overall numerical score of eight for the four bulimia survey items.

Presence of Eating Disorder Bodybuilding Type (EDBT): The six

criteria for a diagnosis of EDBT offered by Gruber and Pope in

their 2000 research were stated in survey questions #5-10

(Appendage E). The Likert scale responses are paired and

assigned numerical values: "Always" and "Usually" (numerical

value of two), "Often" and "Sometimes" (numerical value of

one), "Rarely" or "Never" (numerical value of zero). For a

student-athlete to be diagnosed with EDBT, they must confirm

all six diagnostic criteria by self-reporting a response of

"Always" or "Usually" thereby receiving a numerical score of

twelve for the six EDBT survey items.

Presence of Eating Disorder Not Otherwise Specified (EDNOS):

For a student-athlete to be classified with EDNOS, his anorexia

and bulimia survey responses must display a mixed presentation

(e.g., high endorsement of some anorexia and some bulimia

criteria). The second means to reach an EDNOS diagnosis is to

provide responses that are slightly below the diagnostic

threshold of anorexia or bulimia. With this two approaches, any response less than "Always" and "Usually" (numerical value of two) or greater than "Never" or "Rarely" (numerical value of zero) to a survey question on anorexia or bulimia will default the student-athlete to a diagnosis of EDNOS.

Procedures

Prior to contacting the MAC institutions, the survey protocol was submitted to the University at Buffalo's Social and Behavioral Sciences Institutional Review Board (SBSIRB). Per a SBSIRB's email notification on November 13, 2006 minor changes to the survey were required. The revised survey protocol was resubmitted on January 1, 2007 and was accepted for approval on January 3, 2007.

At that time, the web-based survey became active and telephone calls made to the twelve MAC Directors of Student Athlete Academic Services or the school's Division of Athletics' most comparable position (Appendage I). The initial telephone calls informed the MAC administrator of the purpose of the study and requested the agreement to facilitate the survey.

Upon the school's consent, the contact person received a confirmation and instructional email (Appendage H) that outlined the survey procedures.

Within this email, ten points were addressed: 1) the purpose of the study; 2) the institution's willingness to facilitate the survey; 3) the athletes and sports to be included in the survey; 4) the confidentiality safeguards of the survey, 5) the requirements needed to maintain the survey's degree of confidentially; 6) the exact wording to be emailed to the student-athletes; 7) the survey's website address; 8) the alternate method survey distribution if electronic messaging is not possible; 9) the time-period allowed to complete the survey; and 10) the follow-up timeframe to assess the institution's progress.

The initial email message from the Division of Athletics' representative will encourage their male student-athletes to access the secure survey website that is hyperlinked ('point and clink') to the body of the email message. With this approach, student-athletes can easily open the website from the administrator's email message. Furthermore, the email address of the administrator will most likely be known and familiar to the student-athlete and thereby more likely to be opened and read. To ensure a consistent message with accurate information, the email to student-athlete will be provided to the administrator. If the representative is unable to send an electronic message to their male student-athletes, then head or assistant coaches of all male sport teams should email the instructions to their team. If the coaches are also unable to email their players, the coaches should verbally inform their athletes of the website address and the points of confidentially. Because of a coach's unique position of authority and possible perception of over-involvement in the survey process, this influence has the potential to solicit under-reporting. Consequently, this approach is the least desirable method of facilitating the survey.

Bi-monthly telephone and email follow-up communications occurred via email or telephone correspondences until the institution has reached their end date as stated in the initial email correspondence. These additional bimonthly reminders allowed the institution's contact person to reiterate participation to their male student-athletes. Upon reaching a total sample size acceptable to the faculty committee, thank you letters were sent to the MAC contact persons.

Survey Design. The survey is designed for the student-athletes to self-report their degree of possessing the diagnostic criteria for anorexia, bulimia, EDNOS, and EDBT. The survey begins with statements of purpose and confidentiality. The student-athlete is informed that the survey is about eating, exercise, and compulsive behaviors believed to be present in collegiate athletics. The statement of confidentiality describes the seven safeguards of response confidentially. To advance to the questionnaire, the student-athlete must first agree that they have read the statement of confidentially and give their informed consent. If the student-athlete chooses to not participated, he will be redirected to the official MAC website (www.mac-sports.com).

Upon giving informed consent, the survey begins with

four demographic questions (survey questions #1-4 as seen in

Appendage D). The two questions (institution and sport) are

needed to assess the participation rate of the school and teams.

More importantly, the selection of the latter will determine the

prevalence rate of eating disorders among each sport. The third

and fourth questions (race and grade point average) were initial

variables intended to substantiate or challenge existing research

that certain races are more prone to develop an eating disorder

and eating disorders often result in lower academic

performance. However, with a committee member's direction

and approval, research questions on race or academic

performance were not pursued.

Survey questions #5-10 determines the sample's

presence of Gruber and Pope's (2000) EDBT category. The next

section of the survey lists the DSM-IV's criteria for anorexia

(#11-13) and bulimia (#14-17) in a question format. The last

survey page offers a statement of appreciation, reasserts the confidentiality of the participant's responses, and confirms the

submission of the responses.

Survey Confidentiality Safeguards. Given the stigma

and shame associated with eating disorders (particularly among

males), the survey's high degree of confidentiality is stated in all

communications (the researcher, MAC school contact, and

survey). This repetition is intended to lessen the rate of

underestimated responses. The following seven points of

confidentially are prepared and will be present in all

communications to the sample population:

1. Subjects must given their informed consent to begin the survey.
2. Participation in the survey is voluntary. Refusing to participate is without risk of penalty from school administrators or coaches.
3. The survey is designed so the student-athlete cannot submit his name, email address or any other personal information.
4. The survey can be terminated at anytime without penalty.
5. Responses are anonymous - not to be seen by school administrators, coaches, teammates or family members.
6. Encryption software ensures privacy of participant information.
7. No record can link participant identities with the survey data.

Analysis

Research Question One. *"Among male varsity student-athletes who compete in the Mid-American Conference, what is the presence of anorexia and bulimia as defined by the American Psychiatric Association (2004) and EDBT as defined by Gruber and Pope's 2000 research?"*

Statistical Analysis. A frequency run in SPSS determined the sample's anorexia, bulimia, and EDBT rates of prevalence (See Tables 1-6) and Figures 4-6). To determine if the differences between the anorexia, bulimia, and EDBT means were statistically significant, a paired-sample t-test was conducted using SPSS (See Tables 4.7 – 4.9)

Research Question Two: *"Among male varsity student-athletes who compete in the Mid-American Conference, will the EDNOS category be the most common clinical eating disorder by exceeding the sample's occurrences of anorexia and bulimia?"*

Statistical Analysis. SPSS compared each student-athlete's anorexia and bulimia scores to those category's maximum / cut-off scores. To represent the APA's first EDNOS parameter that symptoms "fall just below the diagnostic threshold [of anorexia or bulimia]," (APA, 1994, p.4) a student-athlete meet this diagnostic parameter with an anorexia or bulimia survey response below "always" or "usually" (numerical value of two) but above "rarely" or "never" (numerical value of zero). With a response score range of zero to two, the lowest a score of one for this parameter still indicates a one-third endorsement of the anorexia criteria and a 25% endorsement of the bulimia criteria. To measure the APA's second parameter for EDNOS of displaying a "mixed presentation" of anorexia and bulimia criteria, a response greater than "never" or "rarely" (numerical value of zero) to more than one survey items for both anorexia and bulimia survey criteria would default the student-athlete to EDNOS (See Tables 4.10 – 4.12).

Research Question Three: "Among male varsity student-athletes who compete in the Mid-American Conference, will the sample's sport be correlated to the presence of anorexia, bulimia, EDNOS, or EDBT?"

Statistical Analysis. A one-way ANOVA was conducted

using each category's (anorexia, bulimia, ENDOS, and EDBT)

"total eating disorder score" as the dependent variable. The

total eating disorder score ranged from zero to thirteen and is

derived from the summation of the anorexia, bulimia, and EDBT

survey response scores (Table 2). To determine if the student-

athlete's chosen sport increased the likelihood of an eating

disorder, an ANOVA (Levene's Test) compared the four sport

groups with the means of the diagnostic survey items. In this

test, alpha was set at 0.05; this is the standard value used to

determine if a statistical significance exists (Table 11). Based on

the result of the ANOVA, a Post-Hoc test was issued to

determine the reliability of the EDBT scale.

CHAPTER IV: RESULTS AND ANALYSIS OF THE DATA

Introduction

This quantitative study examined the three clinical categories from the American Psychiatric Association (APA) used to define an eating disorder. A provisional category identified by compulsive exercise and eating behaviors was also considered (Gruber & Pope, 2000). The sample consisted of 111 male student-athletes that participated in Division I-A athletics in the Mid-American Conference league during the fall 2006 and spring 2007 semesters. Strong emphasis was placed on the "not otherwise specified" category. This clinical, but residual category, is the most common form of an eating disorder (Norring & Palmer, 2005) and the most frequently prescribed eating disorder by clinicians (Golden, et al., 2003), yet it is often ignored in research.

Per the American Psychiatric Association's 1994 Diagnostic and Statistical Manual of Mental Disorders (DSM-IV), the eating disorder "not otherwise specified" (EDNOS) category is intended for clinically severe eating disorder behaviors with symptoms not represented within the diagnostic criteria sets of anorexia and bulimia. As a residual category, EDNOS is a clinical eating disorder for those with anorexic or bulimic symptoms below those categories' diagnostic thresholds or for persons displaying an atypical or mixed presentation of anorexia or bulimia criteria (APA, 2004, p. 4).

The significance of EDNOS as a clinical eating disorder is twofold. First, EDNOS' diagnostic leniency allows for the diagnosis of those displaying clinically severe eating disorder behaviors that would not fall within the diagnostic jurisdiction of anorexia or bulimia (APA, 1994, p. 4). Secondly, this inclusive means to diagnosis is favorable in detecting ill males. In most respects, the high rates of EDNOS among men are the result of this gender's tendency to practice a combination of both anorexic and bulimic behaviors – rarely adhering to only one criteria set for an extended period of time (Schwartz, 2006). Ill males will often keep within the definitions of anorexia and bulimia, but without the behavioral frequency required by the APA (Ackard, Fulkerson, & Neumark-Sztainer, 2006; Woodside, et al., 2005). Since males seldom met the full criteria sets of anorexia or bulimia, the "not otherwise specified" category is often the only means for ill males to receive an eating disorder diagnosis.

With the APA's 1994 release of the DSM-IV and the "not otherwise specified" category, findings of high EDNOS rates began to surface in the late 1990s. The introduction of these studies documented noticeably high gender-neutral eating disorder prevalence rates. The inclusion of EDNOS contradicted the long-standing research approach of only examining anorexia and bulimia. Since these two diseases had become so ingrained and coupled with the association of an eating disorder, the inclusion of the "not otherwise specified" category was short-lived.

In the majority of studies that only tested for anorexia and bulimia insignificant prevalence rates were produced among males since that gender rarely achieves their diagnostic requirements. As a result, these nominal rates of anorexia and bulimia among males are often represented as the gender's complete eating disorder prevalence rate. With the EDNOS category frequently excluded from research, these prevalence calculations do not represent the three categories that define a clinical eating disorder. Consequently, false assumptions on males and eating disorders are inferred. As a model for this practice, even the APA's DSM-IV cites the American eating disorder prevalence rate of both genders derived from occurrences of anorexia and bulimia (APA, 2004). Although the publication states higher rates of prevalence are found in the "not otherwise specified" category, this internationally accepted medical guide indirectly endorses the exclusion of EDNOS to researchers, clinicians, and educators. This published rate the highly regarded authority on mental illnesses has assisted in creating a gender stereotype that further advances the social and medical bias of an eating disorder and physician's low degree of suspicion among males. As a consequence of scores of research excluding the APA's third eating disorder category, society holds a low tolerance in detecting ill males with this disease. For the undetected population, symptoms quickly worsen, serve as mental barrier to stress, and progress into a set of behaviors that one becomes dependent upon.

Males do have negligible rates of anorexia and bulimia, but translating this verity into an unmitigated assumption that "exempts" an entire gender is an inappropriate evolution. This stance ignores the high EDNOS rates consistently found among samples of males. Even with these findings documented, most researchers will exclude the "not otherwise specified" category by favoring the exclusive study of anorexia and bulimia. Perhaps, this divide originates from the precedent of a small number of studies incorporating EDNOS as a research component, the category's residual and anomalous state, or EDNOS's lack of a defined criterion set.

An added obstacle further dissuading EDNOS' inclusion has been the general acceptance of the term "disordered eating." This casual and subjectively used term was conceived in the mid-1990s by the necessity to classify those with eating disorder symptoms and behaviors that did not fall within the DSM-IV's definitions of anorexia or bulimia. This is the obvious intent of EDNOS. Within studies and literature on eating disorders it is common for authors to note low rates of anorexia and bulimia with high findings of "disordered eating." This casual language allows researchers to categorize a section of their sample (sizable at times) that displays abnormal behaviors with food and exercise. In doing so, the intent of EDNOS is sidestepped. Precluding the "not otherwise specified" category in favor of a loosely used term causes misleading prevalence rates by disregarding probable EDNOS diagnoses. This dissolute practice of applying a casual term to ill non-anorexic and non-bulimic populations has weakened the necessity, familiarity, and worth of EDNOS; for "disorder eating" likens these populations to merely having a diet gone awry instead of being tested and appropriately diagnosed with a serious disease that requires professional intervention.

When discussing EDNOS, the category's significance to males and reversing the bias held against them cannot be overemphasized. Excluding EDNOS from its equal anorexia and bulimia counterparts has predetermined ill males with the improbable likelihood of ever being identified. If researchers

began including EDNOS with greater frequency, detected

occurrences of males with eating disorders would increase. By

controlling for all three clinical categories, not just anorexia and

bulimia, a more accurate male prevalence rate would be

revealed. A greater prevalence of males would challenged the

eating disorder myths and stigmas placed on the male gender

while defying the biased environment that surrounds a male in

disclosing his symptoms and behaviors.

Research Findings

Motivated by the importance of the above-stated

considerations and their social implications, a quantitative study

was conducted that surveyed 111 Division I-A college male

student-athletes from nine member institutions of the NCAA's

Mid-American Conference (MAC). Bowling Green State

University and the University at Buffalo agreed to facilitate the

survey, but failed to distribute the assessment to their male

athletes. Western Michigan University declined to participate.

With 111 student-athlete's responses collected and coded,

three research questions were examined using the Statistical

Package for the Social Sciences (SPSS).

  Research Question One: *"Among male varsity student-*

athletes who compete in the Mid-American Conference, what is

the presence of anorexia and bulimia as defined by the

American Psychiatric Association (2004) and EDBT as defined by

Gruber and Pope's 2000 research?"

  Among 96 valid cases, a frequency run determined the

sample's anorexia, bulimia, and EDBT rates of presence. The

survey's three Likert scale paired responses were assigned

numerical values of zero, one, and two (Table 1). The sum of

these assigned values provided the maximum / cut-off scores

for each eating disorder category. These scores for anorexia,

bulimia, and EDBT identified subjects that met a category's

diagnostic criteria. With the survey questions grouped by eating

disorder, the student-athlete's score for a disorder was

produced from their responses to selected survey items. A

frequency run administered by SPSS determined the sample's

presence of anorexia, bulimia, and EDBT.

Table 1

Paired Responses and Corresponding Numerical Values

Paired Response	Numerical Value
"Never" or "Rarely"	0
"Sometimes" or "Often"	1
"Always" or "Usually"	2

A student-athlete would meet a category's maximum / cut-off

score by responding with the most positive paired response of

"always" or "usually" to each of the criteria of a category. The

maximum / cut-off scores are derived from a category's number

of diagnostic criteria multiplied by the numerical value of two.

The numerical value of two is the score of the most positive

paired response that endorses an eating disorder criterion in

the survey. The three criteria for anorexia and four bulimia criteria were taken directly from the DSM-IV (APA, 1994 pp.

589, 594). The six eating disorder "bodybuilding type" criteria

were adopted from Gruber and Pope's (2000) research. Only

matching numerical values of a category's maximum / cut-off

score and the corresponding survey score to that particular

category would categorize a student-athlete with anorexia,

bulimia, or EDBT. Table 2 lists the three categories in question

with their maximum / cut-off scores and value of the most

positive paired survey response of "always" or "usually."

Table 2

Criteria and Response Values to Determine the Maximum / Cut-Off Scores

Category	Number of Criteria	Response Value for "Always" & "Usually"	Maximum / Cut- Off Score
Anorexia	3	2	6
Bulimia	4	2	8
EDBT	6	2	12

As an example of this procedure to categorize, the DSM-IV requires three criteria for a male to be considered anorexic (APA, 1994, p. 589). In the survey administered to 111 student-athletes, one subject replied with answers of "always" or "usually" to each of the three anorexia criteria in the survey. With a value of two assigned to a response of "always" or "usually," his total score for the anorexia portion of the survey was six. This score (six) matches the maximum / cut-off score for anorexia – the value produced by multiplying the value of two for most positive response by the number of the category's criteria. For a listing of the numerical values of each survey response and the three anorexia criteria per the APA that were used in the student-athlete survey see Table 3.

Table 3

Anorexia: Criteria, Responses with Corresponding Values, and Diagnostic Maximum / Cut-Off Score (APA, 1994, p. 589)

Anorexia Criteria	Paired Responses & Corresponding Scores		
	"Always" or "Usually"	"Often" or "Sometimes"	"Rarely" or "Never"
Do you take steps to maintain your body weight at or below a minimal weight for your age and height?	2	1	0
Do you experience an intense fear of gaining weight or becoming fat even though you are underweight?	2	1	0
Do you have a distributed image of your body weight or shape or deny your low body weight?	2	1	0
Maximum / Diagnostic Cut-Off Score	6		

Testing for Anorexia among the Sample. Analysis of the data via a frequency run revealed one case of anorexia producing a 0.9% anorexic prevalence rate. Four student-athletes attained a score of five, falling slightly below the anorexic maximum / diagnostic cut-off score of six and thereby satisfying the EDNOS requirement. Aside from the one anorexic student, the remaining 95 subjects were placed in a "non-

anorexic" group. Fifteen students-athletes did not fully respond

to the three survey items.

Table 4

Frequencies for the Presence of Anorexia, Bulimia, and EDBT

	Missing Cases	No Disorder Displayed	Disorder Displayed
	N	N	N
Athletes Exhibiting Anorexia	15	95	1
Athletes Exhibiting Bulimia	18	93	0
Athletes Exhibiting EDBT	15	96	0

Testing for Bulimia among the Sample. The frequency

run that used the bulimia survey data revealed that that none of

the subjects reached the maximum / cut-off score of eight that

was needed for a classification of bulimia. A quarter of the

sample endorsed some bulimic behaviors as 25.7% received a

score of one or two. When considering the valid data, 18

student-athletes chose not to respond to all four survey questions on bulimia. This high non-response rate led to the assumption of an under-estimated bulimic prevalence rate. To reach and support this assumption, authors of similar studies have found student samples partly completed questionnaires on eating disorder behaviors if they participated in a structured college athletic program (Elliot et al., 2004; Engel et al., 2003; Striegel-Moore & Smolak, 2001; Hausenblaus & Carron, 1999; Sundgot-Borgen, 1999). This presumption from these authors was student-athletes may choose to skip a survey item(s) that they displayed based on the perceived fear of punishment by a coach or college administrator.

Testing for EDBT among the Sample. Two restrictions were encounter with the eating disorder "bodybuilding type" (EDBT) category from a lack of available research on the category. First, all of EDBT's six criteria needed to be endorsed for a positive diagnosis; and secondly, the EDBT scores that were slightly below the category's diagnostic threshold could not be categorized as EDNOS. Even though 56% of the student-athlete sample endorsed four and five of the six "bodybuilding type" criteria, no occurrences of EDBT or EDNOS could be reported. With none of the 111 student-athletes submitting a response of "always" or "usually" to all six criteria, a zero prevalence rate was attained. Furthermore, the response data from the EDBT survey items could not be considered for an EDNOS diagnoses. Even with EDNOS' residual means of accepting behaviors that fall below a category's diagnostic threshold, EDBT's non-clinical status prohibited the data to be considered for a diagnosis of "not otherwise specified" (APA, 1994, p. 4). As a result of EDBT being an unrecognized, non-clinical eating disorder, 56% of the student-athletes that held an EDBT score slightly below the category's maximum / cut-off score could not be represented statistically.

Aside from the APA's requirement that an EDNOS diagnosis can only be derived from anorexia and bulimia, with the recent introduction of the "bodybuilding type" category, not only is it without APA recognition, but research studies and theoretical perspectives are quite limited. Given the absence of any EDBT guidelines or perspectives on conducting a valid test in a quantitative study, the category's diagnostic threshold of six criteria would remain consistent with the APA's provision for anorexia and bulimia. With the APA's specification that all criteria must be endorsed for a diagnosis, the subjectivity in issuing EDBT diagnoses was removed. However, a student-athlete was required to submit a response of "always" or "usually" to *all six EDBT criteria* for a diagnosis. This comparatively high number of criteria relative to anorexia or bulimia caused the absence of any EDBT cases. With a high degree of difficulty to attain the maximum / cut off score, the 56% of student-athletes that regularly engaged in four or five of the six disordered behaviors need to be classified as having normal eating and exercising behaviors.

Even without an EDBT occurrence, significance is found in 56% of the sample highly endorsing the regular practice of four and five of EDBT's six criteria. This finding, although irrelevant to the first research question, is a strong indicator that combinations of EDBT behaviors are used with regularity by male collegiate athletes participating in a wide range of sports. Nonetheless, reporting an absence of EDBT among the sample is statistically accurate, but misleading.

In examining the EDBT histogram, it is apparent that a dominate number of response scores from the EDBT survey items are positioned toward the middle and end of Figure 5. This distribution indicates that a predominance of the sample endorsed most of EDBT's six criteria. The opposite is true when comparing this output to the anorexia and bulimia histograms. In these figures, the greater part of the overall scores is clustered close to zero, producing an abnormal distribution. By comparison, the reverse is observed with the EDBT responses. Since the sample endorsed most of EDBT's criteria, a histogram with a more normal distribution is produced.

EDBT Paired Sample t test and Correlation. Although there was an absence of any EDBT cases, the mean score from the sample's responses to the "bodybuilding type" criteria was much higher than the mean response scores for the anorexia and bulimia survey items. Descriptive statistics via SPSS produced mean scores of 1.33 for anorexia and 1.17 for bulimia.

A higher EDBT mean score of 3.89 was produced. Even though

none of the student-athletes highly endorsed all six EDBT survey

items, a comparison of the means via a paired sample t test

provided a strong indication that EDBT behaviors are far more

prevalent among the sample then anorexic or bulimic

behaviors.

To determine if the differences between the anorexia,

bulimia, and EDBT means were statistically significant, a paired-

sample t test was conducted using SPSS. The first pair tested

compared the anorexia and EDBT means. The bulimia and EDBT

means were the second pair tested. Both paired-sample t tests

determined statistically significant differences did exist between

the anorexia and bulimia scores when compared to the EDBT

scores. These results were plausible based on the large

differences in the means. With averages of 1.33 and 1.17 for

anorexia and bulimia, both are comparable; yet the EDBT mean

of 3.89 is three times greater, indicating a significant variance in

the sample's survey responses. Consistent with this observation, it can be inferred from the paired-sample *t* test that EDBT

behaviors are far more problematic among the sample then

anorexia and bulimia behaviors.

Table 5

EDBT Compared to Bulimia and Anorexia

	Mean	Std. Deviation	Std. Error Mean	*T*	Sig.
Anorexia	1.32	1.61	0.17	-10.93	.0001
EDBT	3.84	2.52	0.026		
Bulimia	1.17	1.25	0.13	-10.14	.0001
EDBT	3.83	2.55	0.27		

Research Question Two: "*Among male varsity student-*

athletes who compete in the Mid-American Conference, will the

EDNOS category be the most common clinical eating disorder by

exceeding the sample's occurrences of anorexia and bulimia?"

Abiding by the APA's parameters for an EDNOS

diagnosis, a 52.5% "not otherwise specified" prevalence rate was attaining from the sample. This rate was determined with

overall anorexia and bulimia scores that fell slightly below those

categories' diagnostic maximum / cut off scores and with the

partial endorsement of both anorexia and bulimia criteria (APA,

1994, p. 4). With over half of a college student-athlete male

sample meeting the standard for a clinical eating disorder, this

finding is has a clear significance to higher education;

specifically to colleges and universities with a male student-

athlete population competing in a structured varsity athletic

program. A varsity team is defined as the principal team

representing the institution in organized sport competitions, as

it is distinctly different in culture and membership from a club

or recreational team.

Specific to the second research question, SPSS

compared each student-athlete's anorexia and bulimia scores to

those category's maximum / cut-off scores. To represent the

APA's first EDNOS parameter that symptoms "fall just below the

diagnostic threshold [of anorexia or bulimia]," (APA, 1994, p. 4)

a student-athlete meet this diagnostic parameter with an

anorexia or bulimia survey response below "always" or

"usually" (numerical value of two) but above "rarely" or "never"

(numerical value of zero). With a response score range of zero

to two, the lowest a score of one for this parameter still

indicates a one-third endorsement of the anorexia criteria and a

25% endorsement of the bulimia criteria. To measure the APA's

second parameter for EDNOS of displaying a "mixed

presentation" of anorexia and bulimia criteria, a response

greater than "never" or "rarely" (numerical value of zero) to

more than one survey items for both anorexia and bulimia

survey criteria would default the student-athlete to EDNOS.

Table 6

Defaulting to EDNOS: Score Range of Anorexia and Bulimia Survey Items

Eating Disorder	Number of DSM-IV Criteria	Score Range to Default to EDNOS	Minimum Score for EDNOS	Maximum Score for EDNOS
Anorexia	Three	Two – Five	Two	Five
Bulimia	Four	Two – Seven	Two	Seven

Note. The "Minimum Score for EDNOS" column is the positive endorsement of one anorexia or bulimia DSM-IV criterion. The "Maximum Score for EDNOS" column is the positive endorsement of all but one anorexia or bulimia DSM-IV criterion.

Note. Only three of the four anorexia criteria stated in the DSM-IV are applicable to males. The criterion excluded from the survey was "In postmenarchal females, amenorrhea i.e., the absence of at least three consecutive cycles" (APA, 1994, p. 589).

With a Likert scale used for the paired responses in the survey, the highest positive endorsement was the selection of "always" or "usually". Either of these responses to any survey item (i.e., a diagnostic criterion) produced the maximum response score of two. The last two columns of Table 6 lists the minimum and maximum scores for an EDNOS diagnosis derived from the overall score earned from the anorexia or bulimia

portion of the survey. As per the DSM-IV, these score were only

derived from the anorexia and bulimia categories (APA, 1994, p.

594). The maximum anorexic and bulimic scores needed to

reach an EDNOS diagnosis were one numerical value less than

those categories' total number of criteria multiplied by the

numerical value of two, i.e., the value given to the highest

positive endorsement of either "always" or "usually". If all the

criteria for anorexia or bulimia had been positively endorsed,

the student-athlete's overall score would equal the category's

total number of criteria multiplied by two. These maximum

scores (six for anorexia and eight for bulimia) are the highest

possible numerical scores of these categories. In this situation

of a subject selecting the most positive response ("always" or

"usually") to all of the category's criteria, the student would be

classified as anorexic or bulimic, not EDNOS.

Testing for EDNOS among the Sample. The sample's

prevalence rate of the "not otherwise specified" category was

determined by following the parameters set by the APA and

listed in the DSM-IV whereas subjects were considered if they

fell slightly below the diagnostic thresholds or displayed a

mixture of the anorexia and bulimia criteria. Determining the

EDNOS prevalence rate was based on the numerical values

discussed in the above section. With this process, 51 student-

athletes from a sample of 97 met the APA's parameters for a

diagnosis of EDNOS, producing an EDNOS prevalence rate of

52.5%. Table 7 indicates the origin of the sample's EDNOS

diagnosis while Table 8 provides the frequency of the anorexia

and bulimia scores within the EDNOS population.

Table 7

Origin of EDNOS Diagnoses among the Sample

EDNOS Origin	Frequency
Via Anorexia Criterion	24
Via Bulimia Criterion	12
Both Categories (Anorexia & Bulimia)	15

Note. The first two columns represent the DSM-IV's first parameter for
EDNOS of displaying slightly less severe or less frequent anorexic or bulimic
symptoms (APA, 1994, p. 4). The last column "both categories (anorexia &
bulimia)" represents the DSM-IV's second EDNOS parameter of displaying a
mixture of anorexic and bulimic behaviors (APA, 1994, p. 4).

Table 8

Frequency of Anorexia and Bulimia Scores Defaulting to EDNOS

Response Score	Anorexia Frequency	Bulimia Frequency
Score of Two	15	13
Score of Three	14	7
Score of Four	6	6
Score of Five	4	1
Score of Six	N/A (Would be anorexic)	0
Score of Seven	-	0
Score of Eight	-	N/A (Would be bulimic)

This study's foremost intent is to advocate for the regular inclusion of the "not otherwise specified" category among eating disorder research. If the conventional method of determining an eating disorder prevalence rate for this sample was followed, the EDNOS category would have been excluded. This would result in 51 student-athletes remaining undetected even as their behaviors meet the provisions for a clinical eating disorder. By only testing for anorexia and bulimia, a 0.9% eating disorder prevalence rate would have been produced from the one case of anorexia. By excluding the EDNOS category, the low prevalent rate would have supported the popular majority belief that eating disorders are not a significant issue for males.

By properly controlling for the three categories that comprise a eating disorder, 53.4% of the student-athletes met the APA's criteria for a clinical eating disorder as all but one fell within the EDNOS category. This finding reinforces the need for researcher to collectively include the EDNOS category; not only because it holds an equal status to anorexia and bulimia, but to detect ill males that would otherwise remain undetected.

Research Question Three. *"Among male varsity student-athletes who compete in the Mid-American Conference, will the sample's sport be correlated to the presence of anorexia, bulimia, EDNOS, or EDBT?"*

By examining the sports from the valid cases of student-athlete responses, only the sports of baseball and football had a sufficient number of survey responses. Therefore, the combination of track and swimming produced an adequate sample size to establish a third category. The combination of these two sports was needed to form a robust category that would not statistically collapse. Merging the responses from athletes that participated in these two sports is reasonable since theorists accept track and swimming as similar sports via their "lean-sport type" classification - sports whereas athletes attempt to maintain a lean physique to excel. Aside from baseball, football, combined track (track / field and cross-country), and swimming there were twelve student-athletes in the sample that did participate in these sports. To include represent the behaviors in the research questions, a fourth sport category ("Other") held the twelve athlete's "total eating disorder score." These student-athletes could not be placed into one of the three existing sport categories since the sport they participated in did not generate enough responses among all nine schools surveyed. Also, these sports did not belong to an establish sport-type category of "lean-based", "weight-restricted", or "appearance-based". With four sport categories established, each group was assigned a numerical value.

Table 9

Sport Category Numerical Label and Number of Student-Athletes

Numerical Label	Sport Category	N
1	Baseball	29
2	Football	28
3	Track/Swimming	22
4	Other	12

Analysis of Variance Test Results. To resolve the third research question, a one-way ANOVA was conducted using each categories' (anorexia, bulimia, ENDOS, and EDBT) "total eating disorder score" as the dependent variable. The total eating disorder score ranged from zero to thirteen and is derived from the summation of the anorexia, bulimia, and EDBT survey response scores. For example, a student-athlete that submitted an "always" or "usually" (response value of two) to the thirteen eating disorder criteria in the survey would produce the highest survey score of 26 that could be attained.

Table 10

Number of Survey Items (DSM-IV Criteria) per Eating Disorder and Maximum Eating Disorder Score

Eating Disorder Category	Number of Survey Items (Diagnostic Criteria)
EDBT	Six Criterions
Bulimia	Four Criterions
Anorexia	Three Criterions
Total Number of Criteria	*Thirteen*
Maximum Eating Disorder Score	*Twenty-Six*

Note. The "Maximum Eating Disorder Score" is the derivative of multiplying the total number of all diagnostic survey items (13) by the numerical value of two – the maximum score potentially received by submitting the most positive response to a survey item, which is a response of "always" or "usually".

From the ANOVA computation, Table 11 displays the means and standard deviations of each category with a numerical range of zero to 26 for the "total eating disorder score." A higher mean indicates the athletes within the sport category responded with higher endorsements to the diagnostic eating disorder survey items.

Table 11

*Mean Eating Disorder Score by Major Sport: Range of Eating
Disorder Scores (Zero to 26)*

Sport	N	Mean	Std. Deviation	F	Sig.
Baseball	29	6.5172	3.91536	0.306	0.821
Football	28	6.4643	3.73653		
Track / Swimming	22	6.0455	5.06601		
Other	12	5.2500	4.13686		
Total	91	6.2198	4.14944		

As shown in Table 11 with a maximum score of 26 the
student-athletes that participated in baseball held a mean of
6.52, with a similar average to football players that produced an
average survey response score of 6.46. The measure of
variability for track / swimming (5.066) was larger than the
baseball and football; two sports with comparable standard
deviations (3.915 and 3.736 respectively). Given the average
mean of 6.21 from all sports, the standard deviations for
baseball and football (3.915 and 3.736) are relatively large.

To determine if the student-athlete's chosen sport increased the likelihood of an eating disorder, an ANOVA (Levene's Test) compared the four sport groups with the means of the diagnostic survey items. In this test, alpha was set at 0.05; this is the standard value used to determine if a statistical significance exists. The ANOVA produced a P-value (0.821) higher then alpha (0.05). With a P-value greater then 0.05 (alpha), the ANOVA determined there was not any statistical evidence to support the assumption that the sample's chosen sport was a factor in eating disorder occurrences. With the result of equal variances, the assumption was met of the ANOVA being a fair test.

A Post-Hoc test determined the reliability of the EDBT scale. To identify each variable in SPSS, numerical labels was assigned: a label of "1" for anorexia; a label of "2" for bulimia; a label of "3" for EDBT; a label of "4" for EDNOS; and a label of "5" for normal behaviors. A numerical score of one represented a positive correlation, as zero denoted normal behaviors.

Table 12

Numerical Labels for Categories of Eating

Category of Eating	Numerical Label
Anorexia	1
Bulimia	2
EDBT	3
EDNOS	4
Normal Behaviors	5

With an alpha of 0.959, the EDBT's six survey items suggest a high reliability - indicating the scale was a good and reliable measure. With the same Post-Hoc test, good reliability with a robust measure was also found for the anorexia scale with an alpha of 0.953. This score indicates the measure was consistent, as most responses to the three criteria were similar. With an alpha of 0.736, the bulimia reliability test was satisfactory. The overall scale of reliability produced an alpha score of 0.969, indicating consistent responses.

Summary

The first research question examined the sample's presence of anorexia, bulimia, and EDBT. One subject attained a maximum / cut-off score for one of these categories with a single case of anorexia detected. Despite these low or absent rates for anorexia and bulimia the eating disorder "bodybuilding type" survey results provided beneficial data that indicated a majority of the student-athlete sample frequently practices the "disordered eating" and exercising behaviors put forward by Gruber and Pope (2000).

To further discuss this point, even without any EDBT occurrences, 56% of the sample regularly practiced four or five of Gruber and Pope's (2000) six EDBT behaviors. This is a strong indication that a high degree of abnormal eating and exercising behaviors exist among the sample - behaviors far more prevalent then anorexic and bulimic behaviors. In comparing the sample's mean responses for the anorexia, bulimia, and EDBT survey items via a paired sample t test, the differences in the responses were found to be "statistically significant."

Considering 56% of the sample reported habitual practices of most EDBT behaviors and 52.5% of the sample met the criteria for EDNOS through the partial or mixed display of anorexia and bulimia criteria, it became clear that this sample of male student-athletes routinely practice a variation of clinical and non-clinical eating disorder behaviors.

Even with this finding, the absence of any EDBT studies or articles to guide a valid test led to a misleading "bodybuilding type" prevalence rate. To maintain a consistent approach to the APA's diagnostic processes for anorexia and bulimia, the positive endorsement of all six EDBT criteria was required. With a relatively high number of behaviors to be endorsed, none of the 111 student-athletes met the rigid EDBT diagnostic threshold. Despite the high number of regularly practiced EDBT behaviors reported, this statistic could not be included in the EDBT prevalence rate.

The decision for the EDBT diagnosis process to remain consistent with the APA's standards was the cause of this misleading result. The lack of any research or discussion beyond

Gruber and Pope's (2000) initial study was a clear limitation in effectively controlling for EDBT in this quantitative study. For EDBT to be a viable research option and still keep the category's integrity and intent, a guiding principle is needed. Possible solutions may include the reduction of EDBT criteria by preserving three or four criteria essential to the category's intent. With this change, the number of "bodybuilding type" diagnostic measures would become consistent to anorexia and bulimia. A second recommendation is the provision to allow a leniency to diagnose with affirmations below the highest endorsement of all six criteria. This lower threshold from a diagnostic leniency would have better represented the "disordered eating" and exercising population in this study that displayed a majority of behaviors central to the category. In adopting this recommendation, the higher amount of EDBT occurrences may begin to distinguish this population that engages in behaviors that will likely led to the onset of a clinical eating disorder. Either of these modifications would have validated the 56% of this sample's behaviors as disordered.

Instead, the majority of the sample that regularly engages in four and five of the six "disordered eating" and exercising behaviors are without any diagnosis and falsely considered to have normal exercising and eating behaviors even though they mirror the category's definition as depict by Gruber and Pope's research (2000).

As an aside, this high frequency of EDBT criteria embodies the findings from other studies that found exercise to be an underlying component of eating disorders. Often, research on compulsive exercise will lead to a part of the sample being casually labeled as having "disordered exercising" behaviors. The high findings of abnormal exercising behaviors, specifically among male athletes, have been coupled to eating disorder detection (Hall & Ostroff, 1998; Yates, 1991; Anderson, 1990; Costin, 1997; Pope, Phillips & Olivardia, 2002; Luciano, 2000; Klein, 1993; Phillips, 2005; Anderson, 1990; Fussell, 1992; Claiborn & Pedrick, 2002; Andersen, Cohn & Holbrook, 2000; Paterson, 2004). The premise of these studies is eating disordered males are drawn to exercise in the same way ill females are motivated to be thin. A substantiation of this correlation via additional empirical research may aid physician, clinicians, practitioners, and athletic staff to recognize exercise dependency as a clear risk factor of eating disorders in males.

The second research question yielded an EDNOS prevalence rate of 52.5%. As required by the APA, these 51 student-athletes had either: 1) a mixture of anorexic and bulimic behaviors, or 2) slightly less severe or frequent anorexic or bulimic symptoms. By exceeding the single occurrence of anorexia, the "not otherwise specified" category was the most prevalent clinical eating disorder in the sample. This result was expected as EDNOS' accommodating nature routinely produces comparably high occurrence rates.

A broader interpretation of the second research question's finding could be made by considering the variation of the eating disorder prevalence rate when EDNOS is excluded. By applying the traditional research approach of only testing for anorexia and bulimia there would have been a similar finding to most eating disorder studies with a minimal (0.9%) male prevalence rate. This rate of occurrence would have supported the common assumption that eating disorders among males with are rare. Conversely, with EDNOS included, a 53.4% clinical eating disorder prevalence rate is found. By obtaining a 52.5% EDNOS prevalence rate, one that is comparable to other studies, research on incorporating the EDNOS category gains further credibility.

Although EDNOS is not a "popular" eating disorder, the category's significance and promise to males and eating disorder etiology is of great consequence. If parallels continue to emerge, the validity of an eating disorder presence should become dependent on including the "not otherwise specified" category.

This study's finding of EDNOS, as with the findings of similar studies, have all identified eating disorders among competitive male athletes as high, only their presence of anorexia and bulimia is low. This different perspective, although true, may be the most difficult to be accepted; for the misperceptions of males and eating disorders are deeply embedded within the western culture. Even with the first documented case of anorexia detected in a young boy, eating disorders are assumed to be a "female disease" of choice, a coping method for some gay men, or a diet gone array. With most eating disordered persons having average or high boy weights, the second assumption of an emaciated and undernourished girl that sees herself as overweight does not represent the majority – only the extreme cases of one eating disorder category (anorexia).

As articulated in this research that considered almost 300 studies, pathogenic and maladaptive eating and / or exercising behaviors from both genders occur in masses, mostly within the college environment – a "breeding ground" as described by (Natenshon, 1999). Although most of these behaviors may not meet the DSM-IV's criteria for anorexia or bulimia, their serious individual and social implications befall upon on higher education.

CHAPTER V: IMPLICATIONS, LIMITATIONS, AND RECOMMENDATIONS

Introduction

By examining specific diagnostic behaviors from a sample of 111 male student-athletes in the Mid-American Conference Division I-A sport league, the finding of a 53.4% eating disorder prevalence rate is a cause for concern. With only one case of anorexia found, 51 student-athletes from a sample of 97 met the clinical criteria for the eating disorder "not otherwise specified" category. Compared to the national male rates for anorexia and bulimia, this rate of presence is extremely high, yet it is comparable to the EDNOS prevalence rates found in other studies. With this, it is fitting for the final chapter of this study to address the implications of these research findings on higher education and the unique position of the male college student-athlete. To a lesser extent, the limitations of this study are discussed as are the recommendations for forthcoming studies.

Three research questions served as a guide to direct this study:

1. Among male varsity student-athletes who compete in the Mid-American Conference, what is the presence of anorexia and bulimia as defined by the American Psychiatric Association (2004) and EDBT as determined by Gruber and Pope's 2000 research?

2. Among male varsity student-athletes who compete in the Mid-American Conference, will the EDNOS category be the most common clinical eating disorder by exceeding the sample's occurrences of anorexia and bulimia?

3. Among male varsity student-athletes who compete in the Mid-American Conference, will the sample's sport be correlated to the presence of anorexia, bulimia, EDNOS, or EDBT?

Discussion of the Findings

Research Question One

By incorporating the anorexia, bulimia, and EDBT survey

data of 96 valid cases into SPSS, a frequency run determined the

sample had one nominal occurrence of these three categories.

The test found no cases of bulimia or EDBT and one case of

anorexia. This result yielded an insignificant 0.9% prevalence

rate.

Responses to the Bodybuilding Type Criteria. Negligible

rates for anorexia and bulimia was expected from the

documented findings within scores of studies and literary

articles. Also, the APA states in the DSM-IV that anorexia and

bulimia are rare among males. Therefore, the "bodybuilding

type" category held the most promise to produce a high degree

of occurrences in the categories under examination in the first

research question. This assumption was incorrect, as none of

the subjects met EDBT's diagnostic measures. As discussed in

the Limitations section, the relatively large number of EDBT

criteria and the adherence to APA procedures for a category

unrecognized by the APA prevented a high EDBT prevalence rate.

Another noteworthy finding from the first research question is illustrated in the histogram produced by the EDBT survey responses. By examining Figure 5, it is clear that high numbers of positive endorsements are positioned toward the middle and end of the EDBT histogram. Clustering in these areas indicates a large portion of the sample endorsed most of the six EDBT criteria. This indicator proved to be accurate as 56% of the sample replied with the two most positive survey responses to four and five of the six "bodybuilding type" behaviors.

Even with this majority of endorsements, none of the student-athletes could be categorized with EDBT. Accepting a positive EDBT diagnosis without a positive endorsement to all six criteria would contradict APA procedures. As an unrecognized category, there has been little written on EDBT. Nor has there being any research or research guidelines on conducting a valid and reliable test with EDBT. Without any precedent of leniency to accept an EDBT diagnosis below an endorsement of all six criteria, none of the subjects could be categorized with the new "bodybuilding type" category. This statistical absence creates a misleading representation of most of the student-athlete's behaviors. As a recommendation, a flexible diagnostic measure or a reduction of criteria would have produced an EDBT presence that reflected the sample's behaviors and upheld the category's intent.

Despite this absence of EDBT cases, a paired sample *t* test confirmed a statistical significant difference between the sample's anorexia, bulimia, and EDBT's scores. The large differences of the means (1.33 for anorexia, 1.17 for bulimia, and 6.21 for EDBT) indicated that EDBT behaviors were the most prevalent among the sample.

Under-Reporting of Bulimic Behaviors. In reviewing the first research question's findings, it was slightly unusual to encounter a male anorexic and no cases of bulimia. The APA has established bulimia to be ten-times more prevalent among males and athletes then anorexia (APA, 1994, p. 594). A probable cause for the lack of bulimia cases was the degree of under-reporting. As discussed in the section on Limitations, nineteen percent of 96 student-athletes partially responded to the four bulimia survey items. The frequency of under-reporting on an eating disorder survey with a college athlete sample has been noted by other researchers: Elliot et al. (2004), Engel et al. (2003), Striegel-Moore and Smolak (2001), Hausenblaus and Carron (1999), and Sundgot-Borgen, (1999). These researchers concluded a perceived fear of punishment from a coach or college administrator may cause a portion of a student-athlete sample to occasionally skip questions on eating disorder behaviors that they practice and should have endorsed.

Research Question Two

The second research question determined that the "not otherwise specified" category was the sample's most common clinical eating disorder. This result was expected based on previous research and literature commonly citing high EDNOS occurrences and low anorexia and bulimia male prevalence rates. To uphold APA standards and produce a fair rate, this study's prevalence of EDNOS was calculated only with the data derived from anorexia and bulimia survey responses. With this approach, a rate comparable to similar studies was derived with a method that cannot be challenged on the basis of validity.

By following the APA's procedure on calculating an EDNOS prevalence rate, 52.5% of the sample met the "not otherwise specified" criteria. Using SPSS to analyze the response scores from the anorexia and bulimia survey items, an EDNOS classification was given to student-athletes that displayed a mixed presentation and / or symptoms slightly below the anorexia and bulimia diagnostic criteria. This EDNOS guideline was established in the APA's 1994 release of the DSM-IV. Adhering to the APA's statement that an EDNOS diagnosis could only be derived from anorexia or bulimia criteria all EDBT survey data was excluded from the EDNOS calculation. By eliminating these responses the study upheld the APA's procedure and replicated the method used by similar studies. Aside from maintaining the objectivity of the APA, including the sample's EDBT data in calculating the EDNOS prevalence rate would have produced a much inflated and overstated rate. This increase would have occurred by incorporating the large number (56%) of sample with EDBT survey responses slightly below the "bodybuilding type's" diagnostic threshold. Without a precedent to fairly use EDBT in a qualitative study, an exaggerated 84.8% EDNOS rate would have been produced by including the EDBT response data.

This study's EDNOS prevalence rate extends beyond the scope of the second research question. With 52.5% of the sample's behaviors classified as a clinical eating disorder, much value is added to changing the customary research procedures to include EDNOS when determining a population's eating disorder presence. As a previously described, the long-standing practice of only considering two of the three categories (anorexia and bulimia) that define a clinical eating disorder is educationally and socially inappropriate. Only recently has this precept begun to be challenged with the findings of increased male detection.

To truly determine the presence of an eating disorder in any population, it is a justifiable expectation based in the medical definition that all three clinical categories that define the disease are included. Excluding the "not otherwise specified" category in determining a prevalence rate is equivalent to omitting anorexia or bulimia in one's methodology when testing for an eating disorder prevalence.

With many social and individual consequences, this pattern of exclusion has led to low male prevalence rates and the perception that eating disorders are a "female disease." Using this sample as a working example, the removal of EDNOS would reduce the 53.4% prevalence of clinical eating disorders to an insignificant prevalence rate of 0.9%. Obviously, the rate of 0.9% does not represent the sample's abnormal behaviors with food and exercise, nor does it deliver an accurate representation of the true relationship among male athletes and clinical eating disorders.

Research Question Three

The final research question sought to determine if the sample's chosen sport was correlated to eating disorder occurrences. A one-way ANOVA considered the three sport categories of baseball, football, and track / swimming. The remaining twelve athletes that did not belong to these sports were place into a fourth category, labeled "Other." The student-athletes on baseball and football teams scored similar means of 3.92 and 3.74. The standard deviation for the combined sports of track and swimming was larger than baseball and football with the mean score of 6.21. The higher mean for track / swimming might be attributed to these sports belonging to the categories of "lean-type" and "appearance-based" sports. As discussed in the third chapter, these categories of sports are proven to hold elevated rates of eating disorders. This increase is believed to stem from the performance benefit received by a low body weight and the higher degree of an athlete's body revealed by the sport's uniform. Even with track/swimming's higher mean and alpha set at 0.05, the ANOVA produced a P-value higher than alpha (0.05). Therefore, this test determined that among this particular sample, the student-athlete's sport type and eating disorders occurrences were not related.

Limitations of the Study

By reviewing this study's findings, four main limitations were identified. The first two limitations caused a disregard of the sample's responses to the EDBT survey items. Despite a noteworthy discovery that 56% of the sample gave their highest endorsement to four or five of EDBT's six criteria, this finding could not be included in the EDNOS or EDBT prevalence rates. The third limitation was the high degree of under-reporting on the survey's four items that identified bulimia. Lastly, a low number of survey responses from athletes in dissimilar sports prevented the testing of eating disorder occurrences among all eleven varsity Mid American Conference sports exclusive to males. With an adequate number of responses from students on a MAC football or baseball team, the survey data from athletes in track and swimming were combined to create a much needed third category.

EDBT Data and the EDNOS Prevalence Rate. As previously discussed in this chapter and chapter four, the EDBT survey data was not considered for an EDNOS diagnosis. As per the DSM-IV, an EDNOS diagnosis can only be derived from sub-standard cases of anorexia and bulimia (APA. 1994, p. 594). Therefore the 54 student-athletes falling just below the EDBT maximum / cut-off score could not be reflected in the EDNOS prevalence rate. The inclusion of these 54 sub-EDBT cases would have been an invalid procedure resulting in an inflated and misleading EDNOS prevalence rate. The absence of any EDBT research or literature disallowed a precedent on the best method to quantitatively convey the significance of the high number of EDBT endorsements.

EDBT Endorsements without an EDBT Diagnosis. The second limitation was also prohibitory in representing the student-athlete majority that regularly engages in four and five of the six EDBT behaviors. This limitation occurred in determining the presence of EDBT. As mentioned above, the inadequate amount of research and scholarly articles on EDBT caused two obstacles in achieving a "bodybuilding type" diagnosis. First, to arrive at an EDBT diagnosis, the responder needed to give the most positive endorsements to relatively high number of criteria. The six criteria for the "body building type" classification are disproportionately high as compared to anorexia and bulimia's three and four criteria. Without the precedent of any research that controlled for the newly proposed category, the method of diagnosis was equally paralleled to anorexia and bulimia, but with a more demanding and difficult means of diagnosis.

Although strict when considering EDBT's six diagnostic criteria, the APA implemented process upheld objectivity. The imposed requirement of endorsing all six of the category's measures caused an absence of any EDBT cases by eliminating the majority that endorsed most of the criteria. With 56% of the sample endorsing four or five EDBT criteria, the finding of no

EDBT cases was not representative of the behaviors that the sample regular practices.

In retrospect, the lack of a guiding principle and inadequate information on the EDBT category was a clear limitation. Placing guidelines intended for an APA clinical disease onto a recently proposed category caused the misleading prevalence rate of zero-percent. Consequently, the fundamental intent of the category was lost. Considering this, it is clear that the absence of any EDBT diagnoses is an unfair reflection of the majority of student-athletes that mirrored Gruber and Pope's (2000) definition of EDBT by engaging in nearly all of the below behaviors:

1. Engage in regular episodes of binge eating without purging (examples of purging are: excessive exercise, self-induced vomiting, restriction of food, etc.)
2. Take steps to maintain a low level of body fat (below 12%) accompanied by a desire to maximize muscle mass.
3. Intense fear of gaining fat or losing muscle, even though body fat is below normal, as defined above, and degree of muscularity is far above average.
4. Strict adherence to a rigid diet with at least two of the following features:

      a. At least five meals per day, consumed on a
regular schedule, for example every three
hours.

      b. Meals all consist of high-calorie, high-protein,
low-fat foods or supplements.

      c. A significant amount of time and money is spent
acquiring, preparing and eating these
specialized meals.

5. Disturbance in the way in which one's body composition
is experienced or undue influence of body appearance
on self-evaluation.

6. Social and occupational opportunities are frequently
given up because they interfere with the composition or
timing of meals.

Even though the EDBT category was an ineffective means to
diagnose, including the category provided a strong indication
that the student-athlete sample held many of the "disordered
eating" and exercising behaviors put forward by Gruber and
Pope (2000). Still, it was ineffective to incorporate a category
into the survey that had six criteria and was incapable to default
to EDNOS. As a category unrecognized by the APA, EDBT is
without clear standards to guide a valid test. Therefore, in
considering the current information available on EDBT, this
category is not operationally ready to be controlled for in a

quantitative study. A qualitative approach using Gruber and Pope's (2000) six behaviors may prove to be more indicative of the category's influence and effect. However, the higher degree of underreporting from personal interviews on eating disorder behaviors is inherently flawed. As additional research and literature on EDBT surfaces, ideally from mental health practitioners and clinicians, the validity in researching this category may allow for measurable findings that are reliable and true. Ironically, practitioner and clinician recognition of behaviors that fell outside of clinical eating disorder categories was the APA's justification in developing the EDNOS category.

Under-Reporting of Bulimia Survey Items. Nineteen percent of the sample did not respond to all of the four bulimia survey items, as 92% of these partial responders opted to ignore of the third bulimia criterion: *[Do you engage in}* *"Recurrent inappropriate compensatory behavior in order to prevent weight gain, such as self-induced vomiting; misuse of laxatives, diuretics, enemas, or other medications; fasting; or excessive exercise?"*

These incomplete surveys lowered the number of valid cases. The 19% of partially answered bulimia survey items precluded the student-athlete from a bulimia diagnosis. This under-reporting may indicate a subject's deliberate choice to skip a survey item(s) that reflect his behavior(s). With this, it can be assumed that some cases of bulimia existed but remained undetected.

As discussed and well-cited in this chapter and chapter four, partial survey responses are common with an eating disorder questionnaire and a student-athlete sample. Researchers have found the perceived fear of punishment from coaches and / or administrators will cause some athletes to ignore an eating disorder behavior(s) they practice.

To reduce the frequency of this known practice, administrators and student-athlete were directed to complete the online survey independently and outside of a group setting. Furthermore, seven confidentially safeguards were implemented and repeatedly communicated. Although unfortunate, this limitation was anticipated from a familiarity of similar studies that have encountered partial reporting.

The Response of Student-Athletes from Similar Sports.

The final limitation of this research was the low number of sports represented among the sample. With only an adequate number of responses from two sports (baseball and football) and combining responses from two similar sports (combined track and swimming) the opportunity to examine a correlation among eating disorders and all eleven male MAC sports was not possible. With EDNOS to be considered in this test, a robust sample of diverse sports that are traditionally excluded from eating disorder studies could have offered a different view on an area that is routinely studied with the same grouping of sports (wrestling, gymnastics, combined track, and swimming). Although athletes from all of the eleven sought after sports did respond, only an adequate number of responses to produce valid categories were received from football and basketball players. Consequently, the responses from the two similar sport-types of swimming and track were combined to create a

much needed third category. With an inadequate number of
responses from athletes that participated in dissimilar sports,
testing for this correlation was compromised.

Even with this limitation, the results from the ANOVA
determined the eating disorder rate for swimming (appearance-
based) and track (lean-based) was not significantly greater than
baseball and football. Because of their precedents of elevated
eating disorder rates, swimming and track are frequently
included in studies testing for eating disorders among athletes.
These two sports are known for having elevated rates because
of their sport-type. Conversely, football and baseball are
perceived as low risk sports. Yet because EDNOS was included,
these two sports held prevalence rates not as high, but
comparable to swimming and combined track.

Although the sample consisted of a fair number of
responders, it would have been beneficial for the responses to
come from athletes that participated in dissimilar sports. Often,
only sports in the categories of "lean-based" (cross-country,
track), "appearance-based" (swimming / diving), or "weight-

restricted" (wrestling) are examined. This causes other sports too rarely (if ever) be considered. As attested to in Richard Dick's 1990 survey of 1,445 NCAA student-athletes, "eating disorders are a complex problem often hidden by those suffering from it, no sport should be considered 'exempt' from the problem" (p. 1). The inclusion of all eleven male varsity sports common among MAC schools would have allowed a test to determine if any correlations existed among eating disorder and sport - regardless of their predetermined "type." Establishing a correlation with sports that are not traditionally studied nor believed to encourage eating disorder behaviors would have challenged the established premise that only sports within a particular category (lean, appearance, or weight-restricted) can serve as a motivator and precursor to the onset of an eating disorder. This belief lowers the suspicion of athletes in sports other then wrestling, swimming, gymnastics, etc. With the high rate of eating disorders from the "not otherwise specified" category, it was likely that athletes from differing sports would hold equal degrees of eating disorder occurrences, thus discrediting a widely accepted belief. Unfortunately, the narrow selection of sports hindered the process of testing for these presumed relationships and production of data to discredit the belief.

Recommendations for Future Studies

The foremost area in need of advanced scholarship is the unique relationship held between males and the "not otherwise specified" category. Decades of research have seldom focused on these two groupings, either separately or together. This exclusionary pattern has led to a significant understudied area of eating disorder etiology and the promotion of social biases. The predominate study of females, anorexia, and bulimia has indirectly formed and augmented eating disorder myths and stigmas; beliefs that are so deeply ingrained within the western culture that clinical judgments and medical diagnoses are biased and hindered.

Advancing knowledge and awareness of the relationship between males and EDNOS will be greatly benefit eating disorder scholarship and provide a more comprehensive understanding of the disease. Presumable outcomes from this evolution in study may produce a greater knowledge of:

1. The EDNOS category and the regard for its clinical standing.

2. Males with eating disorders and their inclination toward EDNOS.

3. A more accurate account of males with eating disorders.

4. The recognized inappropriateness thus decreased use of "disordered eating" as common terminology within eating disorder studies and literature.

By achieving these four outcomes, the stigma surrounding males may be weakened from the increased social awareness that eating disorders is a disease of equally severity to both genders (Norring & Palmer, 2005). With this elevated degree of social acceptance, ill males may become more likely to self-disclose their symptoms. Likewise, physicians and clinicians may be better informed to identify all three eating disorder categories in males and hold a higher tolerance of the disease's gender neutrality. If forthcoming studies continue to agree that predisposing traits are shared among genders and the "not otherwise specified" category gains recognition and clout, the sociological stigmatic view of males with eating disorders may lose credibility as should the sentiments that "people think something must be wrong with a man if he has an eating disorder" (Arnold Anderson in Cohn, 2007).

Aside from aiding social and medical perspectives, the increased understanding and awareness of EDNOS may improve its' credibility and clinical clout. If this were to occur, the validity of eating disorder studies with a general scope (i.e., prevalence / presence of *eating disorders*) should become dependent on the inclusion of the "not otherwise specified category." Albeit far from the current belief, *three categories* define an eating disorder - not just anorexia and bulimia. With this realization, it is reasonable to expect and even call for the inclusion of EDNOS to obtain the true validity of a population's eating disorder presence. With the increased knowledge and appreciation of EDNOS, the contrary of excluding EDNOS should begin to be considered inappropriate and misleading in studies that declared a population's "eating disorder prevalence," when only two-thirds of the disease is represented. In studies that exclude EDNOS, the accurate claim should be the "prevalence of anorexia and bulimia." This statement is both proper and truthful while also acknowledging EDNOS' equal clinical weight to anorexia and bulimia.

If eating disorder research methodology evolved to regularly integrate EDNOS, a direct reduction of the "disordered eating" term should occur. This casual term is used with such regularity that it indicates a significant amount of undetected EDNOS cases. In scores of literature and research findings, authors have side-stepped EDNOS by placing non-anorexic and non-bulimic subjects into a continuum of "disordered eating." Anorexic and bulimic behaviors that are mixed or at the sub-threshold level is the intent and function of EDNOS, yet in most cases the "not otherwise specified" category is excluded and replaced by the casual "disordered eating" term. By excluding the "not otherwise specified" category, the opportunity for these "disordered eating" cases to be considered and potentially diagnosed with a clinical eating disorder has been lost (Bergeron, 2004).

With EDNOS' clinical standing, the category's exclusion in studies and literature is educationally and socially inappropriate with significant consequence. This ongoing and axiomatic practice has lessened eating disorder findings and the rightful regard for EDNOS as a serious diagnostic measure. Exemplifying the extent of normalcy to replace EDNOS for a casual term that is laced with subjectively was quantitatively substantiating this term along side of anorexia and bulimia in the largest study on the presence of eating disorders in college athletics: *Athletes and eating disorders: The national collegiate athletic association study* (Johnson & Powers, 1999). The authors' disregard for EDNOS and use of "disorder eating" improperly repudiated EDNOS' due regard in the exchange of a term with no bearing on a clinical prevalence rate or capacity to diagnosis. With a sample of 1,445 student-athletes, Johnson and Powers (1999) concluded that between 40% and 46% of the sample had "disordered eating." This classification was based on atypical behaviors and patterns of restricting food, body dissatisfaction, and drive for thinness. Johnson and Powers used the student-athlete's demographics, level of athletic involvement, and personality traits as their dependent measures. Even with over 600 colligate student-athletes displaying "disordered eating" behaviors they were never tested for EDNOS, only anorexia and bulimia. Disordered eating, not EDNOS, was determined by the student-athlete's mixed or sub-threshold anorexic and bulimic behaviors. This is the very definition of EDNOS. With the "not otherwise specified" category exempt from the study's methodology, a low eating disorder presence rate was reported to the medical community, the NCAA and the association's 1,281 member institutions. With secondary findings to suggest that elite (Division I-A) athletes' gender, ethnicity, sport, and self-esteem are correlated to behaviors and attitudes of "disordered eating," the finding of 40% to 46% of this large college athlete sample lost that opportunity to bring EDNOS into the national spotlight. Instead, the subject term of "disordered eating" began to be used with more regularity and the large percentage of student-athletes with "disordered eating" did not gain the attention that may have potentially being received with a higher rate of clinical eating disorders.

As a result of studies similar to Johnson and Powers (1999) the regular use of "disordered eating" has been accepted as proper and used with regularity. Unfortunately, because "disordered eating" is a speculative term without a diagnostic measurement, this "disordered eating" population is excluded from all statistical findings of eating disorders presence rates. Often, reports of "disordered eating" and disordered exercising are found ad nauseam within college environment. By failing to notice or choosing to ignore the likelihood of these EDNOS occurrences, the cycle of low eating disorder occurrences among males is socially embedded with a presumed validity. Consequently, colleges and universities do not have reason to respond with a sense of urgency. Yet, the mere placement of a casual label in place of the correct clinical category of EDNOS

will not relive schools with the individual and social implications
of misdiagnosed male populations. Therein lays the value and
significance of further study of the EDNOS category, its effect on
males, and the silent paradox that has befallen on higher
education.

Aside from the recommendation to increase the study
of EDNOS with a male sample and the regular inclusion of the
"not otherwise specified" category within eating disorder
research, Gruber and Pope's (2000) EDBT category is the third
recommendation to be benefited by further study. As discussed
in this chapter's "Limitations" section that called for the
development of a criterion set that is operationally ready,
reliable, and valid for a qualitative study. This would allow the
EDBT category to develop into a reliable predictor of eating
disorders, particularly among males. With theorists and
researchers acknowledging exercise dependency is the
preferred form of purging for male athletes, exercise is often
the underlying expression of this population's eating disorder
(Bamber, Cockerill, Rodgers, & Carroll, 2000). Within the realm

of sports, an athlete's mastery over his body (control) produces a powerful, addicting, and protective shield. Among male athletes, the self discipline needed for this control is both intrinsically and extrinsically revered and rewarded; for this admiration often serves as the kindle that continues to perpetuate the resolute control over self. Cloaking these behaviors to those without the advantage of insight that comes with an intimate personal relationship, the blend of 'male' and 'athlete' allows for a unique social permissibility allowing male athletes to openly engage in and display eating disorder behaviors (Davis, 1992; Rosen, McKeag, Hough, & Curley, 1986).

These acts of well-organized eating and exercise are often mistakenly perceived (by society and him) as noble acts of inner strength through discipline and sacrifice to enhance athletic performance (Thompson & Sherman, 2001). The positive responses from this pretense will often serve as the affirmation that reinforces and justifies his chosen behaviors. From this positive feedback, a strong sense of pride is created and sustained. The influence of this pride as a motivator to continue and increase his chosen behaviors is often unparalleled even by a rise of athletic status. This disparity of the professed reason (athletic performance) versus the true motivator (control) reveals the value that an eating disorder male will place on the "investment" of his behaviors.

Considering that athletic performance often develops into the behavioral justification, this motivator continues to justify behaviors that are strongly embedded into a culture that associates a male's athletic competence to masculinity. With this, athletic status is a valued source of male esteem, standing, and prominence that often rivals intellectual competency and feats. Aside from the motivators of status and prestige that encourage these behaviors, male athlete are seldom dissuaded to change by the medical community, for physicians also hold low degrees of suspicion among eating disorders and males.

With compulsive exercise as the basis for EDBT and the fact that eating disordered males favor exercise as their preferred form of purging, additional research on the "bodybuilding type" category may bring a heightened awareness and regard on the relationship between exercise and male eating disorders. With society's tolerance, rigid exercise by males is an outwardly deceptive behavior. The physical outcome of utilizing EDBT behaviors is also deceptive. Average to high levels of muscular development allows for normal or high body weights with physiques that appear visually healthy (Cororve & Gleaves, 2001).

The modification of EDBT's current criteria set to become research-driven may increase the detection of exercise-driven males from the perception of their eating disorder behaviors from 'accepted and necessary' to 'disordered and evident.' With fewer EDBT criteria or a leniency to diagnostically accept while preserving the category's intent, researchers could better examine the relationship of EDBT's on the onset and continuation of clinical eating disorders. With a research-oriented approach, a useable set of indicators may cause concern for male behaviors currently held in esteem.

Summary

Eating disorders are a significant American health issue worthy of empirical attention on both genders. Yet, a brief search of eating disorder literature will reveal favoritism placed on females, anorexia, and bulimia. Since it is rare for a male to satisfy the diagnostic criteria of anorexia and bulimia, males hold very low prevalence rates for these two diseases. As the prevailing gender, females have garnered a majority of the empirical attention as researchers have examined scores of differing variables on girls and women to better understand the cause and effect of anorexia and bulimia. With this domination of scholarly attention, decades of a disproportionate research has essentially discounted the "not otherwise specified" category and males. As a result, the notion of eating disorders as a "female disease" was established and preserved.

The origin of EDNOS began with the term "atypical" in the APA's 1980 release of the DSM-III (APA, 1980). To a lesser extent, the terms "partial syndrome anorexia" and "partial syndrome bulimia" were also used. The need to include "atypical" into the DSM arose from the inability of the anorexia

and bulimia descriptions to contain all of the abnormal

presentations that were reported by clinicians. The DSM-III

stated the purpose of this "atypical" classification was to

"indicate a category within a class of disorders that is *residual* to

the specific categories in that class" (APA, 1980 & 1987). The

revised version of the DSM-III (APA, 1987) listed three specific

examples (not criteria) of "atypical" eating disorders:

1. A person of average weight who does not have binge-eating episodes, but frequently engages in self-induced vomiting for fear of gaining weight

2. All of the features of Anorexia Nervosa in a female except absence on menses

3. All of the features of Bulimia Nervosa except the frequency of binge-eating episodes.

With the release of the DSM-IV in 1994, the EDNOS category

was formally revealed and reserved for eating disorders of

clinical severity, thereby upgrading the classification of

"atypical" to a category equal in standing to anorexia and

bulimia. As "atypical" evolved into a clinical category, the APA offered a stronger definition for EDNOS. The measures to determine a "not otherwise specified" diagnosis involves two decisive factors. First, there must be a determination of clinical severity; and then, all of the anorexic and bulimic diagnostic criteria are to be unmet. This second measure causes EDNOS to be a diagnosis of exclusion, as EDNOS is without the requirement of any measurable criteria needed to be endorsed (Fairburn & Bohn, 2004). These two factors cause EDNOS to be a residual category because it is dependent on the diagnostic criteria of anorexia and bulimia being unmet (APA, 1994, p. 594). This diagnostic approach is the same for all of the "not otherwise specified" categories in the DSM-IV.

The perception of EDNOS as a residual category may contribute to its' exclusion in research. Secondly, EDNOS is without criteria set, other than the disorder is be considered clinical and not meet the diagnostic standards for anorexia or bulimia via a mixed presentation of both or symptoms that fall below their standards. The benefit of operationally defined criteria in research is an important aspect of research; some may consider clear sets of guidelines as a virtue for exploratory studies. This has also disadvantaged EDNOS from ordinary inclusion in eating disorder studies. Yet, the cost of this practice has resulted in the disregard of the largest category of eating disorders and the exclusion of many potential subjects that differ subtly or heavily from anorexia and bulimia.

Some experts have spoken to the inappropriateness of excluding EDNOS, citing the category is the most common eating disorder diagnosis in clinical practices (Fairburn & Bohn, 2004). Proponents of including EDNOS in research and literature often highlight the category's clinical importance and suggest means to improve its anomalous status. Despite this support, researchers still largely ignored EDNOS and little is written about the category.

In the journal article, *Eating disorder NOS (EDNOS): An example of the troublesome "not otherwise specified" (NOS) category in DSM-IV*, Fairburn and Bohn (2004) sought to add credibility to EDNOS by clarifying its' equal relationship with anorexia and bulimia. As shown in Figure 3, the two overlapping inner circles represent anorexia (the smaller circle) and bulimia

(the larger circle). The area shared by the smaller and larger

circles indicates an endorsement or mixture of both anorexia

and bulimia criteria. In this situation, the DSM-IV has

determined the diagnosis of anorexia will take precedence

(APA, 1994, p. 593). In observing Fairburn and Bohn's

illustration (Figure 3), the outer circle defines what is and is not

an eating disorder though a degree of severity: from clinical

severity to a lesser, non-clinical problem with eating. Within the

outer circle, but outside the two inner circles, represents an

EDNOS diagnosis (Fairburn & Bohn, 2004).

With an absence of a criteria set, it is general

knowledge that the "not otherwise specified" category will

commonly produce higher rates of presence then anorexia or

bulimia. By considering the EDNOS prevalence rates found in

four studies, Fairburn and Bohn (2004) calculated a weighted

EDNOS prevalence rate of 60%. As seen in this study of Division

I-A student-athletes, the combination of males and college

athletics can also produce a comparable EDNOS prevalence rate of 52.5%.

In considering Fairburn and Bohn's (2004) weighted EDNOS average of 60% (Table 13), significance is found in a comparison of the APA's national prevalence rates for anorexia (0.5% to 1%) and bulimia (1% to 3%). (APA, 1994, p. 589). Without citing an EDNOS prevalence rate, only stating the "not otherwise specified" category produces higher occurrences than anorexia and bulimia, the APA claim of one ill male for every ten eating disordered females (APA, 1994, p. 593) losses credibility; for this "ten to one" ratio is another instance of excluding EDNOS from an *eating disorder* rate of prevalence / presence. Omitting EDNOS may be from its residual nature or anomalous state. Yet, it cannot be ignored that the APA's omission of an EDNOS prevalence / presence rate in the DSM-IV contributes to the category's ambiguity and enigmatic state. Medical and public ignorance and misperception of males and eating disorders is a consequence of EDNOS's under-promoted position in eating disorder prevalence.

Table 13

Presence of EDNOS in Samples of Adult Outpatients with Eating Disorders (Fairburn & Bohn, 2004)

Research	Sample Size	Anorexia %	Bulimia %	EDNOS %
Martin et al. (2000)	175	19.4	22.9	**57.7**
Ricca et al. (2001)	189	24.9	24.9	**50.7**
Turner & Bryant-Waugh (2004)	190	5.8	23.7	**70.5**
Fairburn, et al. (in preparation)	121	5.0	33.1	**62.0**
Weighted Average				*60.0*

Note. The prevalence rates of anorexia and bulimia are elevated as compared to the rates listed in the APA because Fairburn and Bohn's samples were taken from researchers with samples of adults with existing conditions of eating disorders and were from in-patient eating disorder treatment centers.

As the understudy of males can be understood from their low rates of anorexia and bulimia, it is difficult to accept the general disregard of EDNOS since category. Accepting EDNOS' residual nature and anomalous state, the category warrants empirical attention since it is the most prescribed eating disorder by clinicians and its' effects are equally severe as anorexia or bulimia (Norring & Palmer, 2005). Still, the category's twenty-year existence pales in comparison to anorexia and bulimia's historical accounts that date back to the 11th century. Perhaps the eclipse of EDNOS is not only derived from its' residual nature or anomalous state, but from history causing the public's familiarity with anorexia and bulimia.

In 1859, anorexia was formally introduced in medical essays, although 11th century narratives of anorexic behaviors caused a divergence among science and religion. Historians agree the origin of anorexia is routed in the Roman Catholic faith, as this religious denomination was used by early followers for eternal salvation through spiritual and physical sacrifice. Early Catholicism renounced material comforts of the "evil corporeal world" and embraced "fasting saints" to lead an austere life as a route to God (Pearce, 2004). This decree of self-discipline was upheld and preached by clergy. Those subscribing to abstinence by self-starvation referenced the duality of mind and body. Detractors accused these believers of hysteria, superstition, and deceit (Pearce, 2004).

The first reported death from anorexia occurred in 383AD as a religious follower of Saint Jerome starved to death (Pearce, 2004). Historical accounts of self-starvation of early female saints and Catholic followers are plentiful as this form of sacrifice was used as a "route to God" (Pearce, 2004, p. 192). Saint Catherine of Siena (1347-1380) died from self-starvation to impart herself to God (Pearce, 2004). Saint Theresa of Avila (1515-1582) also starved herself, using twigs of olives to induce vomiting, and eventually only allowed the Host as her only source of food (Pearce, 2004). (The Host is the "Body of Christ" used in the Sacrament of the Eucharist or Holy Communion – a spiritual feeding symbolic of the Last Supper as the body and blood of Christ is believed to be transformed from bread and wine and received by followers). Saint Mary Axe's (1684) severe anorexic behaviors suppressed her menstrual cycle as her physician observed that "cares and passions of her mind" did not address her failing health (Pearce, 2004). The aspect of control was described by Liles and Woods (1999) account of the historical foundations of anorexia, women, and Catholicism,

> A woman could use the religious starvation to neglect her duties and / or exert some control over others, bargain for sexual abstinence with her husband, reject an unwanted marriage or as a way of praying for her family members. Fasting saints could overpass the authority of the Church men, who followed severe religious practices; they could criticize the religious secular power and authorities and also undertake the role of professors, counselors or reformers of the Church rules, aiming at their own benefit (p. 204).

Although bulimia was first medically reported by physicians Boskind-Lodahl and Gerald Russell in 1976, wealthy men used a vomitorium during the reign of the Roman Empire to self-induce vomiting during gluttonous feasts. In the 19th century, Sigmund Freud addressed bulimia in his medical writings, referring to the disease as a symptom of anorexia motivated by a fear of starvation (Freud, 1926). In 1979, the clinical criterion for bulimia was created by Gerald F.M. Russell, a physician caring for thirty bulimic patients between 1972 and 1978, describing this form of an eating disorder as an "ominous variant" of anorexia (Russell, 1979).

The unfamiliarity of EDNOS is due in part from anorexia and bulimia based on long-standing historical accounts. Nonetheless, EDNOS holds an unparalleled significance to the relationship among eating disorders and males. The equal understanding of anorexia, bulimia, and EDNOS would allow the "not otherwise specified" category to benefit by increased detection and diminished gender bias and social ignorance.

Excluding a category that represents the largest population of diagnosed eating disorders (Fairburn, et al., 2003; Turner & Bryant-Waugh, 2004) from scientific studies can be considered socially and educationally irresponsible.

Furthermore, it is unusual for a residual category to produce the largest grouping of a clinical disorder yet receive minimal attention. It is common for ill persons to fall between categories – meeting the criteria for anorexia or bulimia, then falling below their diagnostic thresholds, classified as EDNOS, and then returns to their original diagnosis. Thus, anorexia and bulimia will change to EDNOS and vice versa. Most eating disorder cases (particularly males) will fall into the EDNOS category. This neglect diminishes the category's regard and lessens the significance of the disease's relationship among males.

Consequently, with anorexia and bulimia set (thus perceived) as the primary forms of eating disorder detection in research, invalid male presence rates and a false understanding of the disease is perpetuated. As long as these beliefs remain unchallenged, males with eating disorders will remain hidden and suffer in isolation. Some males will find a false sense of control through sport or exercise and discover a place that accepts and encourages their extreme behaviors and an unwavering drive. In this environment, their masculinity is linked to performance – an aspect they can control. In this setting, males are encouraged and accepted. This environment becomes the basis of one's identity. Behaviors not understood by those on the "outside" are justified. As eating and exercising behaviors begin to control one's life, the lifestyle becomes an addictive cage without a release; for feelings of normalcy and strength are instantly manufactured that prevent the impression that he is helpless or weak.

FIGURES

Figure 1. The "Eating Continuum" as illustrated in *Life Inside the Thin Cage (*Rhodes, 2003, p.19).

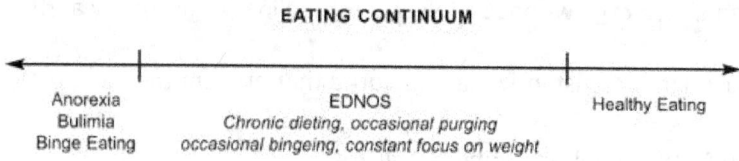

Figure 2. Similarities Between "Good Athlete" Traits and Anorexic Characteristics (Thompson & Sherman, 1999)

"Good Athlete"	"Anorexic Individual"
Mental Toughness	Asceticism
Commitment to Training	Excessive Exercise
Pursuit of Excellence	Perfectionism
Coachabilty	Over-Compliance
Unselfishness	Selflessness
Performance Despite Pain	Denial of Discomfort

Figure 3. Relationship among Anorexia, Bulimia, and EDNOS
(Fairburn & Bohn, 2004)

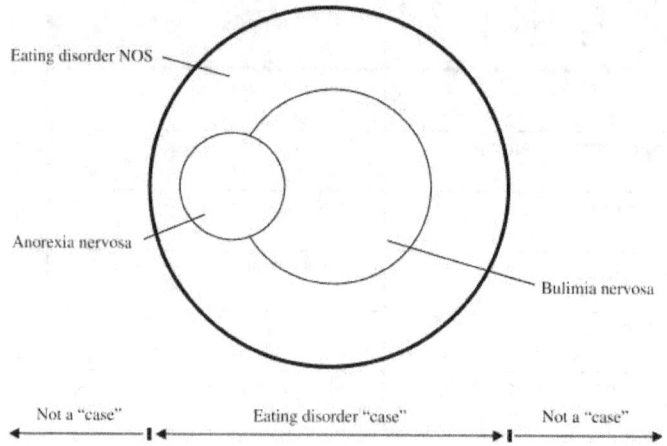

Figure 4. SPSS Output: Sample's Total Anorexia Scores

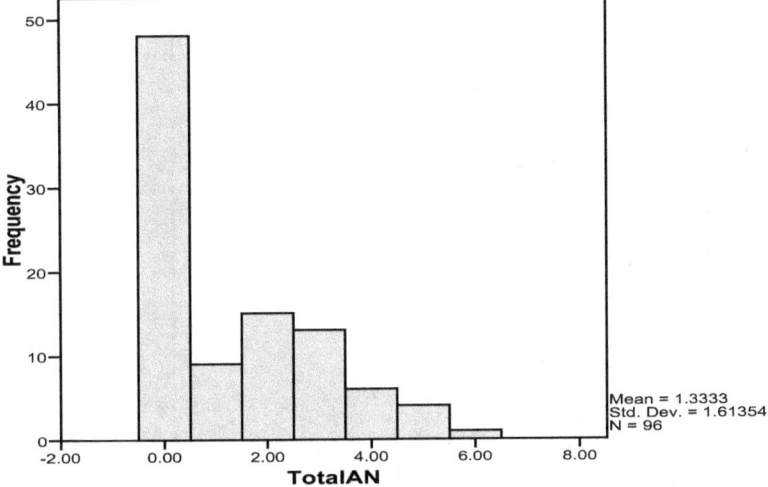

Figure 5. SPSS Output: Sample's Total Bulimia Scores

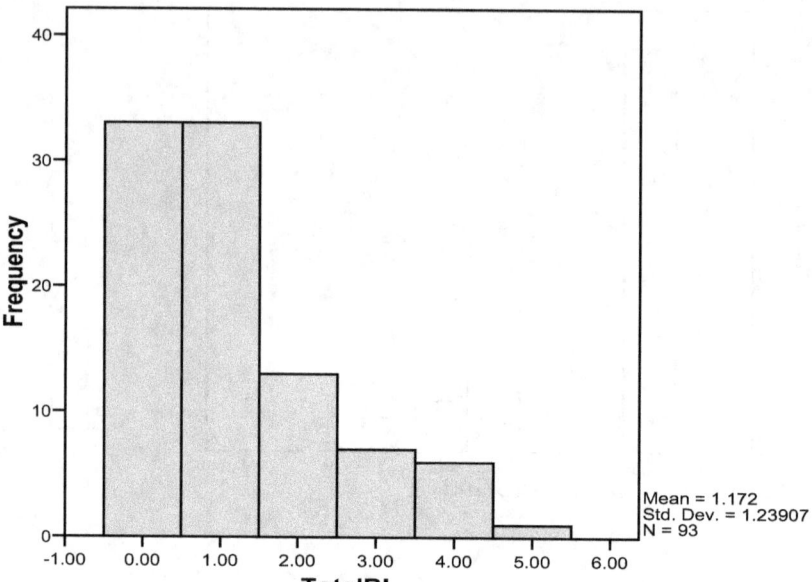

Figure 6. SPSS Output: Sample's Total EDBT Scores

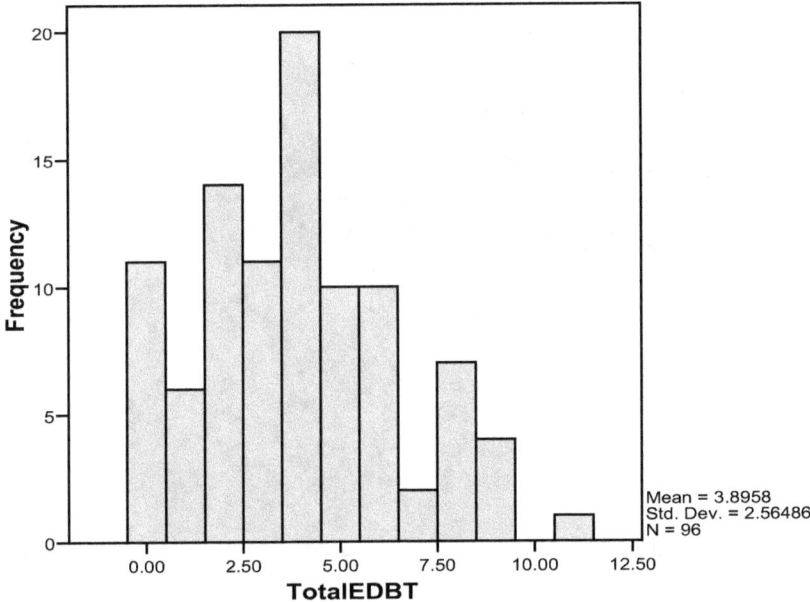

Figure 7. Eating Disorder Contributors (Natenshon, 1999)

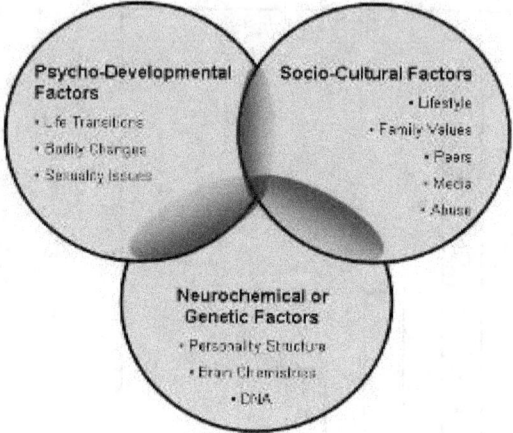

Figure 8. Magazine Advertisement for Animal Hardcore Pack

supplements in <u>Flex Magazine</u>, February, 2004

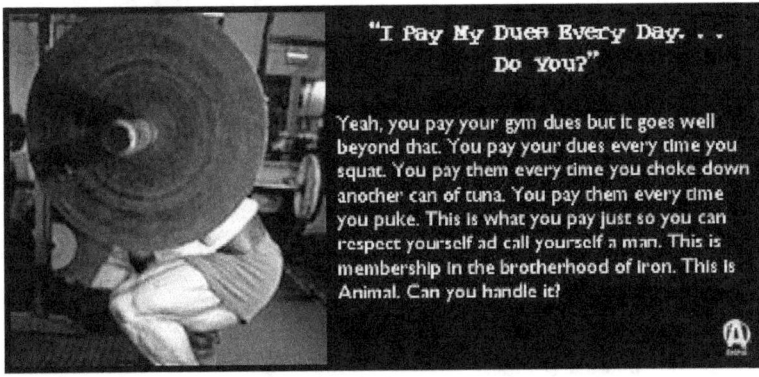

Figure 9. In the article "Obsessive Exercise Is an Overlooked Eating Disorder" James Rippe asserts that colleges are an addictive 'breeding ground' for eating disorders as compulsive and obsessive exercise ranks just behind marijuana use in a survey of college students (Endaya, 2001).

Ranking of Unhealthy Behaviors among College Students
1. Binge Drinking (33.3%)
2. Tobacco Use (31.2%)
3. Marijuana Use (24.8%)
4. Compulsive and Obligatory Exercising (21.3%)
5. Over-the-Counter Stimulants (13.7%)
6. "Club" Drugs (9.8%)
7. Amphetamines (4.5%)
8. Cocaine (2.6%)

APPENDIX A

Mid-American Conference Male Student Demographics for the

2005-2006 Academic Year

Total Undergraduate Student Population	199,291

Average Undergraduate Population	16,607
Highest	*19,668 (Eastern Michigan)*
Lowest	*12,522 (U. of Akron)*
Total Male Undergraduate Population	92,315 (46.3%)
Average Male Undergraduate Population	7,693
Highest	*9,702 (W. Michigan U.)*
Lowest	*5,938 (U. of Akron)*
Total Male Student-Athlete Population	3,019
Average Male Student-Athlete Population	252
Percentage of Male Student-Athletes	*4.63% (U. of Akron)*
Highest	*2.19% (U. of Toledo)*
Lowest	

APPENDIX B

Institutional Sports and Undergraduate Student Demographics

of the Mid-American Conference (2005-2006 Academic Year)

MAC Member Institution	Student Population	Athlete Population	Athlete Population (Male)	Varsity Sports	Varsity Sports (Male)	Male Varsity Sports & Number of Athletes
Ball State University	16,072	462	224 (48.5%)	17	7	Baseball (35) Basketball (14) Football (105) Golf (12) Swimming & Diving (29) Tennis (11) Volleyball (18)
Bowling Green State University	14,730	409	230 (56%)	16	7	Baseball (36) Basketball (13) Football (102) Golf (11) Ice Hockey (29) Soccer (25) Combined Track (14)
Central Michigan University	16,892	411	246 (67%)	12	5	Baseball (37) Basketball (14) Combined Track (16) Football (108) Wrestling (31)
Eastern Michigan University	19,668	570	315 (55%)	17	7	Baseball (39) Basketball (15) Combined Track (155) Football (109) Golf (9) Swimming & Diving (30) Wrestling (28)

APPENDIX B (Continued)

Institutional Sports and Undergraduate Student Demographics
of the Mid-American Conference (2005-2006 Academic Year)

MAC Member Institution	Student Population	Athlete Population	Athlete Population (Male)	Varsity Sports	Varsity Sports (Male)	Male Varsity Sports & Number of Athletes
Ball State University	16,072	462	224 (48.5%)	17	7	Baseball (35) Basketball (14) Football (105) Golf (12) Swimming & Diving (29) Tennis (11) Volleyball (18)
Bowling Green State University	14,730	409	230 (56%)	16	7	Baseball (36) Basketball (13) Football (102) Golf (11) Ice Hockey (29) Soccer (25) Combined Track (14)
Central Michigan University	16,892	411	246 (67%)	12	5	Baseball (37) Basketball (14) Combined Track (16) Football (108) Wrestling (31)
Eastern Michigan University	19,668	570	315 (55%)	17	7	Baseball (39) Basketball (15) Combined Track (155) Football (109) Golf (9) Swimming & Diving (30) Wrestling (28)

APPENDIX B (Continued)

Institutional Sports and Undergraduate Student Demographics
of the Mid-American Conference (2005-2006 Academic Year)

MAC Member Institution	Student Population	Athlete Population	Athlete Population (Male)	Varsity Sports	Varsity Sports (Male)	Male Varsity Sports & Number of Athletes
Ball State University	16,072	462	224 (48.5%)	17	7	Baseball (35) Basketball (14) Football (105) Golf (12) Swimming & Diving (29) Tennis (11) Volleyball (18)
Bowling Green State University	14,730	409	230 (56%)	16	7	Baseball (36) Basketball (13) Football (102) Golf (11) Ice Hockey (29) Soccer (25) Combined Track (14)
Central Michigan University	16,892	411	246 (67%)	12	5	Baseball (37) Basketball (14) Combined Track (16) Football (108) Wrestling (31)
Eastern Michigan University	19,668	570	315 (55%)	17	7	Baseball (39) Basketball (15) Combined Track (155) Football (109) Golf (9) Swimming & Diving (30) Wrestling (28)

APPENDIX C

Student-Athlete Web-Based Survey

Page One: Purpose, Confidentiality, and Informed Consent

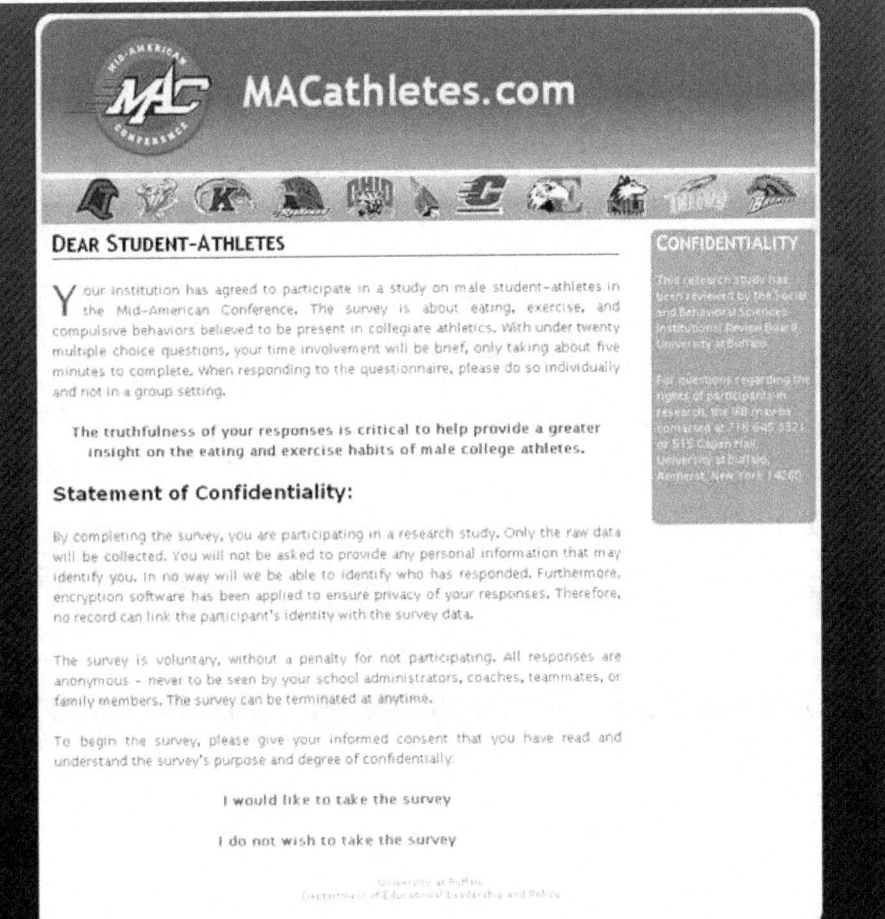

MACathletes.com

DEAR STUDENT-ATHLETES

Your institution has agreed to participate in a study on male student-athletes in the Mid-American Conference. The survey is about eating, exercise, and compulsive behaviors believed to be present in collegiate athletics. With under twenty multiple choice questions, your time involvement will be brief, only taking about five minutes to complete. When responding to the questionnaire, please do so individually and not in a group setting.

The truthfulness of your responses is critical to help provide a greater insight on the eating and exercise habits of male college athletes.

Statement of Confidentiality:

By completing the survey, you are participating in a research study. Only the raw data will be collected. You will not be asked to provide any personal information that may identify you. In no way will we be able to identify who has responded. Furthermore, encryption software has been applied to ensure privacy of your responses. Therefore, no record can link the participant's identity with the survey data.

The survey is voluntary, without a penalty for not participating. All responses are anonymous - never to be seen by your school administrators, coaches, teammates, or family members. The survey can be terminated at anytime.

To begin the survey, please give your informed consent that you have read and understand the survey's purpose and degree of confidentially.

I would like to take the survey

I do not wish to take the survey

University at Buffalo
Department of Educational Leadership and Policy

CONFIDENTIALITY

This research study has been reviewed by the Social and Behavioral Sciences Institutional Review Board, University at Buffalo.

For questions regarding the rights of participants in research, the IRB may be contacted at 716 645 3321, or 515 Capen Hall, University at Buffalo, Amherst, New York 14260.

APPENDIX D

Student-Athlete Web-Based Survey

Page Two: Demographics of Student-Athlete Responders

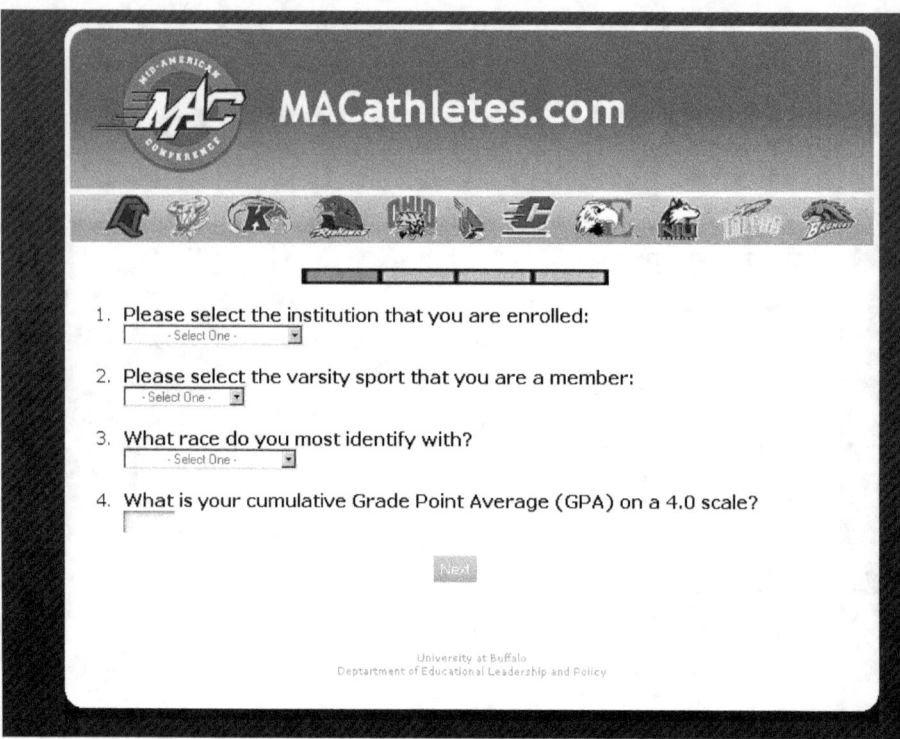

APPENDIX E

Student-Athlete Web-Based Survey

Page Three: Eating Disorder Bodybuilding Type (EDBT) Criteria
(Gruber & Pope, 2000)

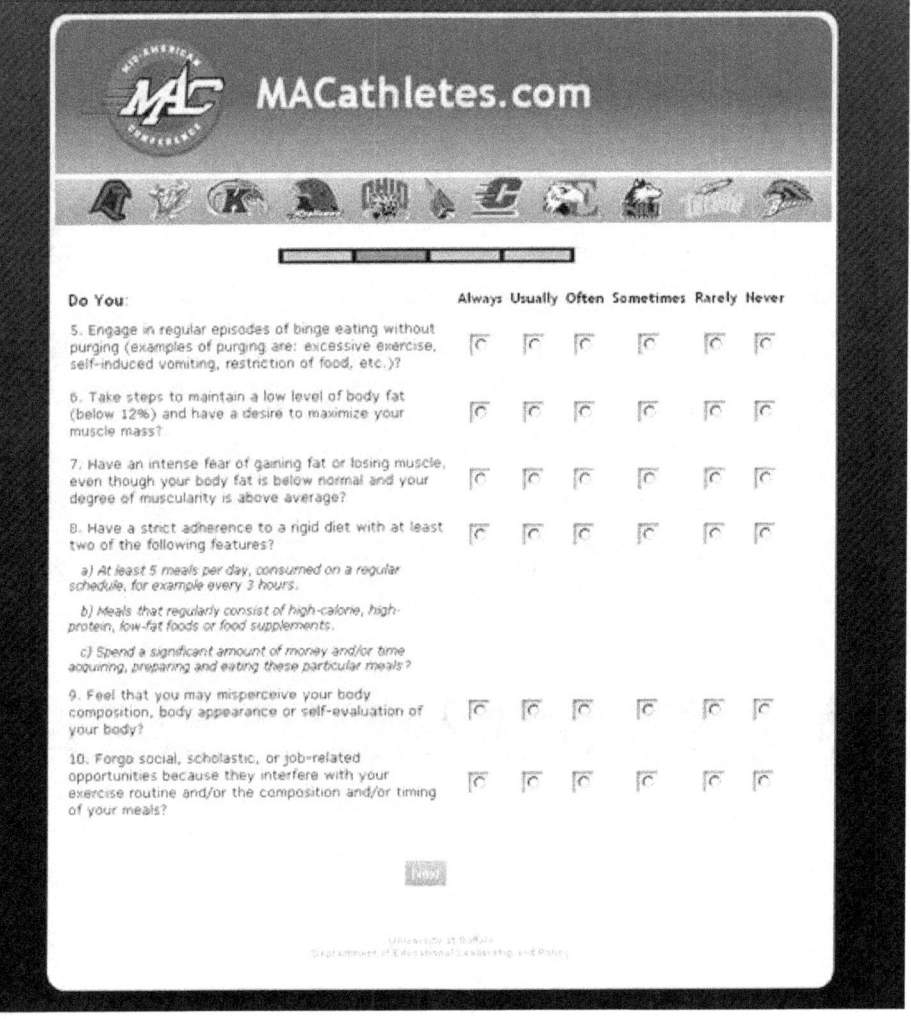

MACathletes.com

Do You:

	Always	Usually	Often	Sometimes	Rarely	Never
5. Engage in regular episodes of binge eating without purging (examples of purging are: excessive exercise, self-induced vomiting, restriction of food, etc.)?	○	○	○	○	○	○
6. Take steps to maintain a low level of body fat (below 12%) and have a desire to maximize your muscle mass?	○	○	○	○	○	○
7. Have an intense fear of gaining fat or losing muscle, even though your body fat is below normal and your degree of muscularity is above average?	○	○	○	○	○	○
8. Have a strict adherence to a rigid diet with at least two of the following features?	○	○	○	○	○	○
a) At least 5 meals per day, consumed on a regular schedule, for example every 3 hours.						
b) Meals that regularly consist of high-calorie, high-protein, low-fat foods or food supplements.						
c) Spend a significant amount of money and/or time acquiring, preparing and eating these particular meals?						
9. Feel that you may misperceive your body composition, body appearance or self-evaluation of your body?	○	○	○	○	○	○
10. Forgo social, scholastic, or job-related opportunities because they interfere with your exercise routine and/or the composition and/or timing of your meals?	○	○	○	○	○	○

Next

University at Buffalo
Department of Educational Leadership and Policy

APPENDIX F

Student-Athlete Web-Based Survey

Page Four: Anorexia Criteria (APA, 2004, p. 589)

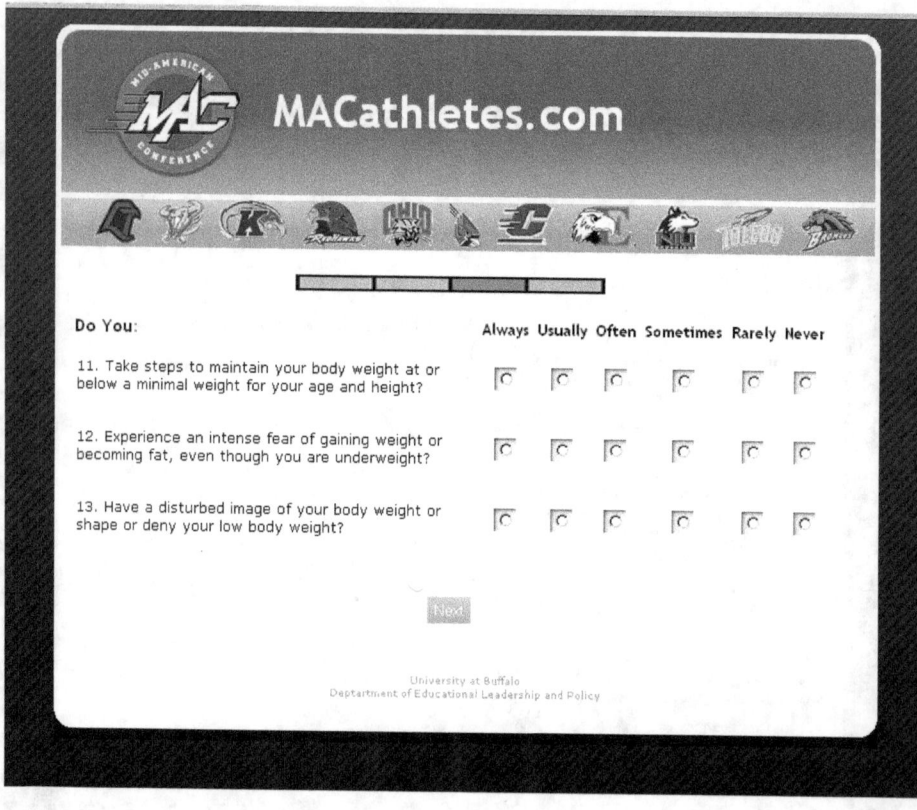

APPENDIX G

Student-Athlete Web-Based Survey

Page Five: Bulimia Criteria (APA, 2004, p. 594)

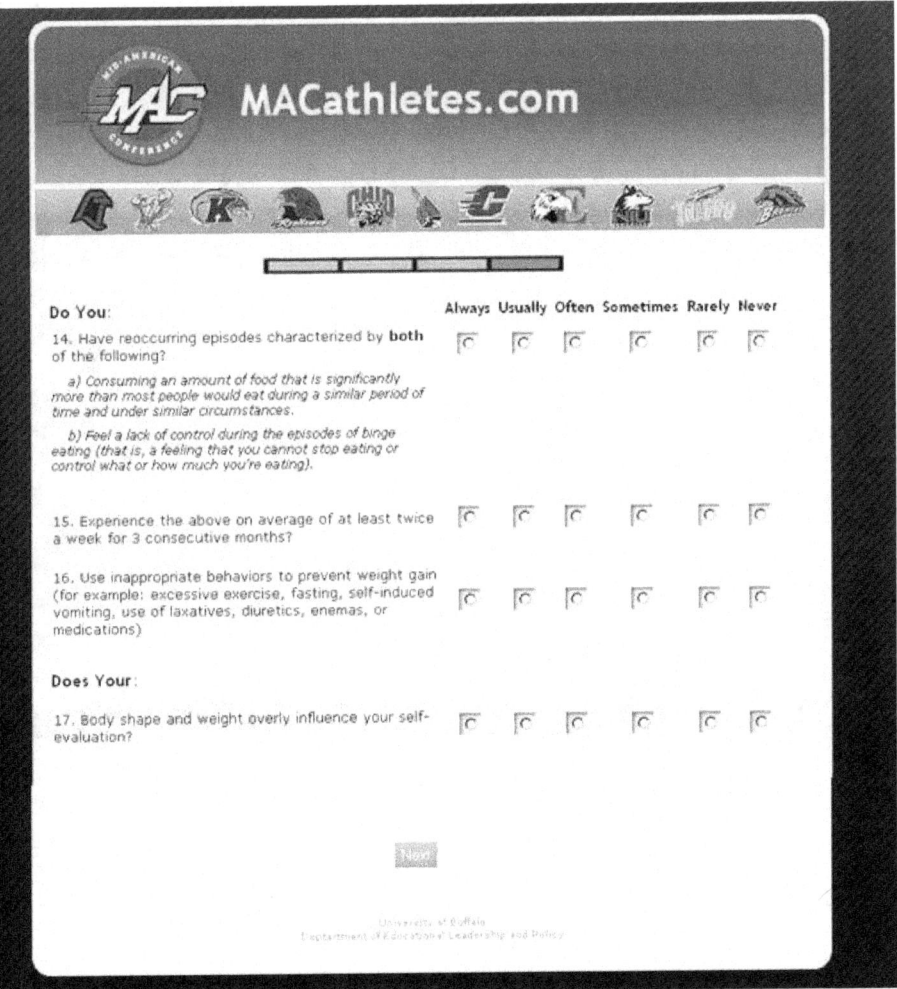

APPENDIX H

Student-Athlete Web-Based Survey

Page Five: Confirmation of Responses as Submitted and Indication of Survey's Conclusion

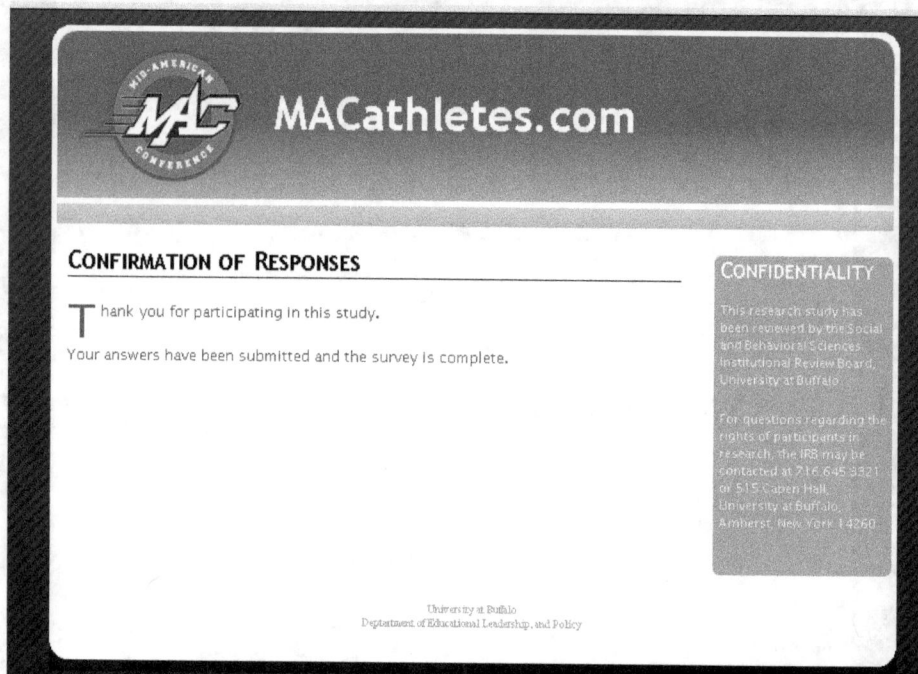

MACathletes.com

CONFIRMATION OF RESPONSES

Thank you for participating in this study.

Your answers have been submitted and the survey is complete.

CONFIDENTIALITY

This research study has been reviewed by the Social and Behavioral Sciences Institutional Review Board, University at Buffalo.

For questions regarding the rights of participants in research, the IRB may be contacted at 716.645.3321 or 515 Capen Hall, University at Buffalo, Amherst, New York 14260.

University at Buffalo
Department of Educational Leadership, and Policy

APPENDIX I

Confirmation and Instructional Email to MAC Administrators

Date	November, 2006
From	'Rob Suglia' <rlsuglia@buffalo.edu>
To	'MAC Representatives'
Subject	MAC MALE-ATHLETE SURVEY

Per our phone conversation, this email provides the instructions to facilitate a survey of your male student-athletes. The responses from your student-athletes are essential in determining the prevalence of a specific eating disorder for a research study.

INSTRUCTIONS

This study is only for male student-athletes in good standing as determined by your institution.

For the student's convenience, the survey is web-based. Therefore, the website address needs to be given to your male athletes. It is preferred that this is done by sending the below email message:

"Our institution has agreed to participate in a study of male student-athletes in the Mid-American Conference. The survey's questions are about your eating and exercise habits.

All of your responses will always be completely confidential - never to be seen by school administrators, coaches, teammates, or family members. This survey is voluntary. There are no penalties for not participating and it can be stopped at any time. Moreover, the survey is designed to eliminate the need for personal information (name, username, email address, etc.). Any type of identification cannot be given nor can responses be traced.

The estimate time commitment is only about 5 minutes (under 20 questions). When responding to the questionnaire, please do so individually and not in a group setting.

Your truthful and timely responses are appreciated. To begin this brief survey, please click on the following website: www.macathletes.com

If you are unable to email your male-athletes, then the head or assistant coaches should email the above message to their team. If this is also impossible, then a coach should verbally inform their athletes of the website address and degree of confidentially. Because of a coach's unique position of authority, they must express the below points:

‣ The survey is designed so that the student-athlete cannot, nor is he required to submit his name, email address, username, or any other personal information.
‣ Responses are anonymous - not to be seen by school administrators, coaches, teammates, or family members.
‣ Participation in the survey is voluntary. Refusing to participate is without risk of penalty from school administrators or coaches.
‣ The survey can be terminated at any time without penalty.
‣ Encryption software ensures privacy of participant information.
‣ No record can link participant identity with the survey data.
‣ The subjects must given their informed consent to begin the survey.

Again, the survey is intentionally designed to preserve confidentially. As part of all your communications (verbal or written), it is crucial that this confidentially is always restated. If you have any questions on the procedures please contact me. I will speak to you in a couple of weeks to follow-up on your institution's progress. Thank you for your assistance with this study that will assist colleges to gain a better understand of their male student-athletes.

APPENDIX J

MAC Institution Contacts to Request Survey Facilitation to the

School's Male Student-Athletes (November, 2006)

Ball State University
Dr. Pamela Riegle
Coordinator for Academic Support Services for Student Athletes
765-285-5426
priegle@bsu.edu

Division of Athletics
North Quad Room 322
2000 W. University Ave.
Muncie, IN 47306

Bowling Green State University
Naomi Lee
Assistant Athletic Director for Student-Athlete Services
419-372-7103
nplee@bgnet.bgsu.edu

Division of Athletics
200 Memorial Hall
Bowling Green, OH 43403

APPENDAGE J (Continued)

MAC Institution Contacts to Request Survey Facilitation to the

School's Male Student-Athletes (November, 2006)

Central Michigan University
Pat Podoll
Assistant Athletics Director for Academics
989-774-6091
pat.podoll@cmich.edu

Division of Athletics
IAC 220
Mount Pleasant, Michigan 48859

Eastern Michigan University
Vaughn, Teiryne
Coordinator of Athletics Certification
734.487.6795
teiryne.vaughn@emich.edu

Division of Athletics
Convocation Center
Ypsilanti, MI 48197

APPENDAGE J (Continued)

MAC Institution Contacts to Request Survey Facilitation to the

School's Male Student-Athletes (November, 2006)

Kent State University
Jen Kulics
Assistant Athletic Director for Academic Services
330-672-2961
jkulics@kent.edu

Division of Athletics
185 MACC
PO Box 5190
Kent, OH 44242

Miami University
Cynthia Verald
Academic Coordinator
513-529-8005
veraldcm@muohio.edu

Division of Athletics
230 Millett Hall
Oxford, OH 45056

APPENDAGE J (Continued)

MAC Institution Contacts to Request Survey Facilitation to the

School's Male Student-Athletes (November, 2006)

Northern Illinois University
Francine St. Clair
Director of Academic Services
815-753-1727
fstclair@niu.edu

Intercollegiate Athletics
Convocation Center
CV 217
Dekalb, IL 60115

Ohio University
Lori Friel
Director of Academic Services
740-593-1172
friell@ohio.edu

Division of Athletics
Athens, OH 45701

APPENDAGE J (Continued)

MAC Institution Contacts to Request Survey Facilitation to the

School's Male Student-Athletes (November, 2006)

<u>University at Buffalo</u>
Kellie Peiper
Student-Athlete Services Coordinator
716-645-6472
kpeiper@buffalo.edu

Division of Athletics
169 Alumni Arena
Buffalo, NY 14260

<u>University of Akron</u>
Tiffany Seoldo
Director of Academic Support Services for Student-Athletes
330-972-8659
tgibson@uakron.edu

Division of Athletics
373 Carroll Street
Rhodes Arena
Akron, OH 44325

APPENDAGE J (Continued)

MAC Institution Contacts to Request Survey Facilitation to the

School's Male Student-Athletes (November, 2006)

University of Toledo
Mike Meade
Assistant Athletic Director for Academics
419-530-3540
mmeade@utnet.utoledo.edu

Division of Athletics
2801 W. Bancroft St.
Toledo, OH 43606

Western Michigan University
Jeff Stone
Associate Athletic Director of Academic and Compliance
Services
269-387-3082
stone@groupwise.wmich.edu

Division of Athletics
1903 W. Michigan Ave.
Kalamazoo, MI 49008-06

References

Academy for Eating Disorders Conference, (2001, May),

Vancouver, Canada and excerpted in *Eating Disorders*

Review, July-August 2001, Gurze Books).

Adkins, E. C. & Keel, P. K. (2005). Does "excessive" or

"compulsive" best describe exercise as a symptom of

bulimia nervosa? *International Journal of Eating*

Disorders(1), 38, 24–29.

Alderman, B., Carlson, J., Landers, D., & Scott, J. (2003). Factors

related to rapid weight loss practices among

international-style wrestlers. *American College of Sports*

Medicine: Medicine and Science in Sport and Exercise.

Alexander, L. (1998, March). The prevalence of eating disorders

and disordered eating behaviors in sororities. *College*

Student Journal, 32(1), 66-75.

American Psychiatric Association (1994). *Diagnostic and*

Statistical Manual of Mental Disorders. 4th ed.

Washington, DC.

Ames-Frankel J., Devlin M, Oldham J., Sadik C., Strasser T., &

Walsh B. (1992). Personality disorder diagnoses in

patients with bulimia nervosa: Clinical correlates and

changes with treatment. *Journal of Clinical Psychiatry,*

53, 90-96.

Anderson, A. (1990). Males with eating disorders.

Brunner/Mazel Eating Disorders Monograph Series.

Anderson, A. (1995, September). Eating disorders in males.

Psychiatric Times.

Andersen, A. (2001). How I practice: Responding to the phrase "I

feel fat." *Eating Disorders: The Journal of Treatment and*

Prevention(8), 167-169.

Andersen, A., Bowers, W., & Watson, T. (2001). A slimming

program for eating disorders not otherwise specified:

Reconceptualizing a confusing residual diagnostic

category. *Psychiatric Clinics of North America, 24,* 271-

280.

Anderson, A., & Mickalide, A. (1983). Anorexia nervosa in the

    male: An under-diagnosed disorder. *Psychosomatics,*

    24, 1067-1075.

Andersen, R. E., Bartlett, S. J., Morgan, G. D.,. & Rowena, K. D.

    (1995). Weight loss, psychological and nutritional

    patterns in competitive male body builders.

    International Journal of Eating Disorders, 18, 49-57.

Anderson, S. Basson C., Geils C. (1997). Personality style and

    mood states associated with a negative addiction to

    running. *Journal of Sports Medicine, 4,* 6–11.

Anorexia Nervosa and Bulimia Association (1997). Men with

    eating disorders. *Reflections: Quarterly Newsletter(2)*3.

Anthony, J., Wood, I., & Goldberg, S. (1982). Determining the

    populations at risk for developing anorexia nervosa

    based on selection of college major. *Psychiatry*

    Research, 7, 53-58.

Baer, J., Walker, W., & Grossman, J. (1995). A disordered eating

    response teams effect on nutrition practices in college

    athletes. *Journal of Athletic Training, 30*(4), 315-317.

Bamber, D. Cockerill, I., & Carroll, D. (2000). The pathological

status of exercise dependence. *British Journal of Sports

Medicine, 34*(2), 126-132.

Bamber, D., Cockerill I., Rodgers S., & Carroll D. (2000). It's

exercise or nothing: A qualitative analysis of exercise

dependence. *British Journal of Sports Medicine, 34*(6):

423-430.

Beals, K., & Manore, M. (1994). The prevalence and

consequences of sub-clinical eating disorders in female

athletes. *International Journal of Sports Nutrition, 4*,

175-195.

Becker A., Grinspoon S., Klibanski A., & Herzog D. (1999). Eating

disorders. *New England Journal of Medicine*, April 8;

340(14), 1092-1098.

Becker A., Keel P., Anderson-Fye E., & Thomas J. (2004). Genes

and/or jeans?: Genetic and socio-cultural contributions

to risk for eating disorders. *Journal of Addictive

Diseases, 23*(3), 81-103.

Benson, J., Alleman, Y., Theintz, G., & Howald, H. (1990). Eating

problems and calorie intake levels in Swiss adolescent

athletes. *International Journal of Sports Medicine, (11),*

249-252.

Berkman J. (1930). Anorexia nervosa: Anorexia, inanition and

low basal metabolic rate. *American Medical Science,*

180, 411–424.

Birtchnell, S., Dolan, B., & Lacey, H. (1987). Body image

distortion in non-eating disordered women.

International Journal of Eating Disorders, 6, 385-391.

Black, D. (Ed.) (1991). Eating disorders among athletes: Theory,

issues, and research. *American Alliance for Health,*

Physical Education, Recreation, and Dance. Reston, VA.

Black, D., & Burckes-Miller, M. (1988). Male and female college

athlete: Use of anorexia nervosa and bulimia nervosa

weight loss methods. *Research of Exercise Sport, 59,*

252-256.

Black, D., Larkin, L., Coster, D., Leverenz, L., & Abood, D. (2003).

   Physiologic screening test for eating

   disorders/disordered eating among female collegiate

   athletes. *Journal of Athletic Training, 38*(4), 286-297.

Blaydon M., Lindner K., & Kerr J. (2002). Metamotivational

   characteristics of eating-disordered and exercise-

   dependent tri-athletes: An application of reversal

   theory. *Psychology of Sport and Exercise, 3*(3), 223-236.

Blinder, B. J. (2001) *Anorexia in Males.* Retrieved December 22,

   2005 from www.ltspeed.com/bjblinder/anmales.htm.

Blumenthal, J., O'Toole, L., and Chang, J. (1984). Is running an

   analogue of anorexia nervosa? *Journal of the American*

   Medical Association, 252, 520-523.

Borgen, J., & Corbin, C. (1987). Eating disorders among female

   athletes. *The Physician and Sports Medicine, 15,* 89-95.

Borresen-Gresko, R. & Karlenson, A. (1994). The Norwegian

   program for the primary, secondary, and tertiary

   prevention of eating disorders. *Eating Disorders: The*

   Journal of Treatment and Prevention, 2, 57-63.

Boyadjieva, S. and Steinhausen, H. C. (1996). The eating attitudes test and the eating disorder inventory in four Bulgarian clinical and non-clinical samples. *International Journal of Eating Disorders(119)*, pp. 93-98.

Brown G. H. (1955). Munk's roll. Lives of the fellows of the royal college of physicians of London (1826–1925). London: *The Royal College of Physicians*, IV: 116–7.

Brownell, K., Rodin, J., & Wilmore, J. H. (1992). Eating, body weight and performance in athletes of modern society. In *Sports Medicine Handbook, 2003 – 2004* (pp. 202 – 221).

Bruch, H. (1979) *Golden Cage: The Enigma of Anorexia Nervosa.* Vintage.

Bruch, H. (1981). Developmental considerations of anorexia nervosa and obesity. *Canadian Journal of Psychiatry, 26,* 212-217.

Burckes-Miller, M., & Black D. (1988). Behaviors and attitudes associated with eating disorders: Perceptions of college athletes about food and weight. *Health Education Theory and Practice, 3,* 203-208.

Burckes-Miller, M., & Black, D. (1988, February-March). Eating disorders: A problem in athletics? *Health Education Research, 3,* 22-23.

Burkes-Miller, M., & Black, D. (1988). Male and female college athletes: Prevalence of anorexia nervosa and bulimia nervosa. *Athletic Training,* 23(2), 137-141.

Button, E. J. (2005). Don't forget EDNOS (eating disorder-not otherwise specified): Patterns of service use in an eating disorders service. *Psychiatric Bulletin,* 29, 134-136.

Carlat, D., Camergo, C., & Herzog, D. (1997, August). Eating disorders in males: A report on 135 patients. *American Journal of Psychiatry,* 154,(8).

Carter, J. (2002, August). *Presentation at the Annual Meeting of the American Psychological Association,* Chicago, IL.

Chronicle of Higher Education: Almanac. Retrieved on December 11, 2005 from

http://chronicle.com/weekly/almanac/2001/nation/010 2001.htm

Cohn, L. (2000). Fat is not just a feminist issue anymore. Making weight: Men's conflicts with food, weight, shape and appearance. In Anderson, A., Cohn, L, & Holbrook, T. (2000). *Making Weight: Men's Conflicts with Food, Weight, Shape and Appearance.* Gürze Books.

Combs, A. (1981). A *Personal Approach to Teaching: Beliefs that Make a Difference.* Boston: Allyn and Bacon.

Cororve, M. B. & Gleaves, D. H. (2001). Body dysmorphic disorder: A review of conceptualizations, assessment, and treatment strategies. *Clinical Psychology Review, 21*(6), 949–970.

Couper, M. P. (2000, Winter). Web surveys a review of issues and approaches. *Public Opinion Quarterly,64*(4), 464-481.

Crisp A.H., & Burns T. (1983). The clinical presentation of

anorexia nervosa in males. *International Journal of*

Eating Disorders, 2(4), 5-10.

Crowther, M., Tennenbaum, D. L., Hobfoll, S.E., & M.A.

Stephens (Eds.). *The Etiology of Bulimia Nervosa: The*

Individual and Familial Context (pp. 1 - 26) Washington,

D.C.: Taylor & Francis.

Crowther, J. H., Wolf, E. M., & Sherwood, N. (1992).

Epidemiology of bulimia nervosa. In M. Crowther, M.,

Tennenbaum, D. L., Hobfoll, S. E. & Stephens, M. A.

(Eds.). *The Etiology of Bulimia Nervosa: The Individual*

and Familial Context (pp. 1 - 26) Washington, D.C.:

Taylor & Francis.

Cruse, W. (2003). Dangerous eating disorders discussed at

special-interest meeting in Indianapolis. *National*

Spotlight. NFHS News, November – December.

Cullari, S., Rohrer, J., & Bahm, C. (1998). Body image

perceptions across sex and age groups. *Perceptual and*

Motor Skills, 87, 839-847.

Davis C. & Cowles M. (1989) A comparison of weight and diet

   concerns and personality factors among female athletes

   and non-athletes. *Journal of Psychosomatic, 33,* 527.

Davis, C., Kennedy, S., Ravelski, E., & Dionne, M. (1994). The role

   of physical activity in the development and

   maintenance of eating disorders. *Psychological*

   Medicine, 24, 957-967.

DePalma, M., Koszewski, M., Case, J., Barile, R., DePalma, B., &

   Oliaro, S. (1993). Weight control practices of light

   weight football players. *Medicine and Science in Sports*

   and Exercise, 694-700.

DePalma, M, Koszewski, W., & Romani, W. (2002). Identifying

   college athletes at risk for pathogenic eating. *Britain*

   Journal of Sports Medicine, 36, 45-50.

Dick, R. (1990, September, 17). NCAA Eating Disorder Survey.

   NCAA News.

Dick, R., Oppliger, R., Scott, J. Utter, A. (1992). Wrestling with

   weight loss: The NCAA wrestling weight management

   policy. *NCAA News.*

Dillman, D. A. (2000). *Mail and Internet Surveys: The Tailored Design Methods*. Second Ed. New York: Wiley.

Dolhanty, J. (1998, February). Giving up an eating disorder: What else might you be giving up? *National Eating Disorders Information Centre Bulletin 13(1)*.

Drewnowski, A., Yee, D. K. (1987). Men and body image: Are males satisfied with their body weight? *Psychosomatic Medicine, 49*, 626-634.

Duda, J., Bernadot, D., & Kim, M. (2004). The perceived gym and parental motivational climate at home and in the gym and psychological precursors of eating disorders among young elite female gymnasts. *The Sport Psychologist.*

Duda, J., Chi, L., Newton, M., Walling, M., & Catley, D. (1995). Task and ego orientation and intrinsic motivation in sport. *International Journal of Sport Psychology, 26*, 40-63.

Dummer, G. M., Rosen, L. W., Heusner, W. W., Roberts, P. J. &

   Cousilman, J. E. (1987). Pathogenic weight-control

   behaviors of young competitive swimmers. *Journal of

   Physicians and Sports Medicine, 15*, 75-86.

Eating Disorder Resources (1999). Athletes and eating disorders:

   Some ramifications of the NCAA study. *Eating Disorders

   Review, 10*(6).

Endaya, D., Obsessive exercise is an overlooked eating disorder.

   Published Thursday, May 3, 2001. Issue 119, Volume 81

   from www.dailynexus.com/article.php?a=958

Engel, S., Johnson, C., Powers, P., Crosby, R., Wonderlick, S.,

   Wottrock, D., & Mitchell, J. (2003). Predictors of

   disordered eating in a sample of elite Division I college

   athletes. *Eating Behaviors, 4*, 334-343.

Elliot, D. L., Goldberg, L, Moe, E. L.; DeFrancesco, C. A., Durham,

M B. & Hix-Small, H. (2004. November). Preventing

substance use and disordered eating initial outcomes of

the athena (athletes targeting healthy exercise and

nutrition alternatives) program. *Archives of Pediatrics*

and Adolescent Medicine, 158.

Fairburn, C. G., Copper, Z. (1993). The eating disorder

estimation. In: Fairburn C. G., Wilson, G. T., (Eds.). *Binge*

Eating: Nature, Assessment, and Treatment. New York,

NY: Guilford Press: 1993: 317-360.

Fitcher, M., & Daser, C. (1987). Symptomology, psychosexual

development and gender identity in 42 anorexic males.

Psychological Medicine, 17, 409-418.

Fredrickson, B., Roberts, T., Noll, S., Quinn, D., & Twenge, J.

(1998). That swimsuit becomes you: Sex differences in

self-objectification, restrained eating, and math

performance. *Journal of Personality and Social*

Psychology, 75, 269-284.

Fries, H. (1977). *Monograph*, Acta Psychiatrica Scandinavica,

248.

Fulkerson, J., Keel, P., Leon, G., & Dorr, T. (1997). Eating-

disordered behaviors and personality characteristics of

high school athletes and non-athletes. *International*

Journal of Eating Disorders, 26, 73-79.

Garber, J., & Brooks-Gunn, J. (1996). Prevention of eating

problems: An 8-year study of adolescent girls.

Developmental Psychology, 30, 823-834.

Garman, J., Hayduck, D., Crider, D., & Hodel, M. (2004).

Occurrence of exercise dependence in a college-aged

population. *Journal of American College Health, 52*(5).

Garner, D. M. (1984). *Research on Eating Disorders and*

Sport/Fitness Participation. Canada.

Garner, D. M. (1991). Eating disorder inventory 2: Professional

manual. *Psychological Assessment Resource,* Odessa, FL.

Garner D. M. (1993). Binge Eating in Anorexia Nervosa. Binge

    Eating: Nature, Assessment and Treatment, (pp. 50 -

    76). C. G. Fairburn & G. T. Wilson (Eds.). New York:

    Guilford Press.

Garner, D. M. (1997). Psychoeducational principles in the

    treatment of eating disorders. In *Handbook for*

    Treatment of Eating Disorders (pp. 145 - 177). D .M.

    Garner & P. E. Garfinkel (Eds.). New York, NY: Guilford

    Press.

Garner, D. M., & Garfinkel, P. E. (1979). The Eating Attitudes

    Test: an index of the symptoms of anorexia nervosa.

    Psychological Medicine, *9*, 273-279.

Garner, D. M., & Garfinkel, P. E. (1980) Sociofactors in the

    development of anorexia nervosa. *Psychological*

    Medicine, 10, 647-656.

Garner, D. M., Garfunkel, P. E., Stancer, H., & Moldofsky, H.

    (1976). Body image disturbances in anorexia nervosa

    and obesity. *Psychosomatic Medicine, 38*, 327-336.

Garner, D. M., Rosen, L., & Barry, D. (1998). Eating disorders in

athletes. *Child and Adolescent Psychiatric Clinics of*

North America, 7.

Gordon, R. A. (2000). *Eating disorders: Anatomy of a social*

epidemic. Blackwell Publishers: 2nd Ed.

Graber, J. A., Brooks-Gunn, J., & Petersen, A. C. (1996).

Adolescent transitions in context. In J. A. Graber, J.,

Brooks-Gunn, J., & Petersen, A. C. (Eds.), *Transitions*

Through Adolescence: Interpersonal Domains and

Context. (pp.369 -3 83). Mahwah, NJ: Erlbaum.

Graham, E. *College men increasingly suffer from eating*

disorders, partly pressured by athletics. Retrieved on

January 2, 2006 from

http://www.dailyprincetonian.com/

Granner M., Abood D, & Black D. (2001). Racial differences in

eating disorder attitudes, cigarette, and alcohol use.

American Journal of Health Behavior 25(2): 83-99.

Gross, J. (2005, April 22). Campus life, survey finds high rate of

eating disorders. *The Daily Princeton.*

Gruber A., & Pope H. (2000). Psychiatric and medical effects of

anabolic-androgenic steroid use in women.

Psychotherapy and Psychosomatics 69(1), 19-26.

Guarda, A. (2001). First Steps to Curb Eating Disorders among

Top Athletes. *American Journal of Psychiatry*. 158, 570-

574.

Gull W. (1874). Anorexia nervosa (apepsia hysterical, anorexia

hysteria). *Transactions of the Clinical Society of London,*

7, 22–28.

Gunn, H. (2002). Web-based surveys: Changing the survey

process. *FirstMonday 7*(12). Retrieved June 2, 2006

from firstmonday.org database.

Gutgesell, M., Moreau, K., & Thompson D. (2003). Weight

concerns, problem eating behaviors, and problem

drinking behaviors in female collegiate athletes. *Journal*

of Athletic Training 38(1), 62-66.

Hamilton, L., Brooks-Gunn, J., & Warren, M. (1985).

Sociolcultural influences on eating disorders in

professional female ballet dancers. *International Journal*

of Eating Disorders, 4(4), 465-477.

Hamilton, L., Brooks-Gunn, J., Warren, M., & Hamilton, W.

(1986, July-August). The impact of thinness and diet on

the professional ballet dancer. *Cahper Journal, 52*(4),

30-35.

Harris, R. (1991). Clinical lectures on diseases of the nervous

system. Translated by *Tavistock Classics in the History of*

Psychiatry.

Harris, M., & Greco, D. (1990). Weight control and weight

concern in competitive female gymnasts. *Journal of*

Sport and Psychology,12, 427-433.

Hasse, A. M. & Prapavessis, H. (2001). Social physique anxiety

and eating attitudes in female athletic and non-athletic

groups. *Journal of Science and Medicine in Sport(44),*

396-405.

Hausenblas, H., & Carron, A. (1999). Eating disorder indices and

   athletes: integration. *Journal of Sport and Exercise*

   Psychology, 21(3), 230-258.

Hausenblas, H. A., & Mack, D. E. (1999). Social physique anxiety

   and eating disorder correlates among female athletic

   and non-athletic populations. *Journal of Sport Behavior,*

   22, 502-524.

Heatherton, T., Mahamedi, F. Stripe, M., & Field, A. (1997). A

   10-year longitudinal study of body weight, dieting, and

   eating disorder symptoms. *Journal of Abnormal*

   Psychology, 106, 117-125.

Heatherton, T., Nichols, P., Mahamedi, F., & Keel, P. (1995).

   Body weight dieting and eating disorder symptoms

   among college students 1982-1992. *American Journal of*

   Psychiatry, 152, 1623-1629.

Hoek, H. W. (1995). The distribution of eating disorders. In K. D.

   Brownell & C. G. Fairburn (Eds.) *Eating Disorders and*

   Obesity: A Comprehensive Handbook (pp. 207-211).

   New York: Guilford.

Holliman, S. C, Ed. (1991). *Handbook for coaches on eating disorder and athletics*. Dubuque, Iowa: Kendall-Hunt Publishing Company.

Hueneman, R., Shapiro, L., Hampton, M., & Mitchell, B. (1966). A longitudinal study of gross body composition and body confirmation and their association with food and activity in a teen-age population. *American Journal of Clinical Nutrition, 18*, 325-338.

Johnson, M. (1994). Disordered eating in active and athletic women. *Clinics in Sports Medicine, 13*(2).

Johnson, C., Crosby, R., Engel, S., Mitchell, J., Powers, P., Wittrock, D., & Wonderlich, S. (2004). Gender, ethnicity, self-esteem and disordered eating among college athletes. *Eating Behaviors*, 5, 147-156.

Johnson, C. & Maddi, K. (1986). The etiology of bulimia: Biopsychosocial perspectives. *Adolescent Psychiatry, 13*, 253-273.

Johnson, C., Powers, P. S., & Dick, R. (1999). Athletes and eating

disorders: The national collegiate athletic association

study. *International Journal of Eating Disorder, 26*(2),

179-188.

Johnson, J., Spitzer, R. (2001). Health problems impairment and

illnesses associated with bulimia nervosa and binge

eating disorder among primary care and obstetric

gynecology patients. *Psychological Medicine, 1*(31), 455-

466.

Katz, J. (1986). Long distance running, anorexia nervosa and

bulimia: Report of the two uses. *Comprehensive*

Psychiatry, 27(1), 74-78.

Katzman, M., & Wolchik, S. (1994, June). Bulimia and binge

eating in college women: A comparison of personality

and behavioral characteristics. *Journal of Consulting and*

Clinical Psychology, 52, 423-428.

Kaye, W .H., Klump, K. L., Frank, & Strober, M. (2000). Anorexia

and bulimia nervosa. *Annual Reviews of Medicine, 51,*

299-313.

Kearney-Cooke, A., & Steichen-Asch, P. (1990). Men, body

    image, and eating disorders. In A. Andersen (Ed.), *Males*

    with Eating Disorders, 47. New York: Brunner/Mazel.

Kelly, J., Patten, S., & Johannes, A. (1982). Analysis of self-

    reported eating and related behaviors in an adolescent

    population. *Nutrition Research, 2*, 417-432.

Kirk, G., Singh, K., & Getz, H. (2002, Fall). Risk of eating disorders

    among female college athletes and non-athletes.

    Journal of College Counseling, 4(2), 122-133.

Kleifield, E., Wagner, S., & Halmi, K. (1996). Cognitive-behavioral

    treatment of anorexia nervosa. *Psychiatric Clinic of*

    North America, 19, 715-737.

Knapp, C. (2003). *Appetites: Why women want.* Counterpoint

    Press.

Knowlton, L. (1995, September). Eating disorders in males.

    Psychiatric Times, 12(9).

Kostar, E. (1993). Eating disorders: Gymnasts at risk.

    International Gymnast, 25(11). 58-59.

Krane, V., Waldron, J., Stiles-Shipley, J., & Michalenok, J. (2001).

Relationships among body satisfaction, social physique

anxiety, and eating behaviors in female athletes and

exercisers. *Journal of Sport Behavior, 24*(3).

Krosnick, J. A. & Chang, L. (2001). *A comparison of the random

digit dialing telephone survey methodology with

internet survey methodology as implemented by

knowledge networks and Harris Interactive.* Retrieved

on June 2, 2006 from http://www.psy.ohio-

state.edu/social/krosnick.htm

Krueger, J., & Clement, R. (1994). The truly false consensus

effect: An ineradicable and egocentric bias in social

perception. *Journal of Personality and Social

Psychology, 67,* 596–610.

Lane, A. M. (2003). Relationships between attitudes toward

eating disorders and mood among student athletes.

Journal of Science and Medicine in Sport, 66, 144-154.

Lasegue, C. (1873). De l'anorexie hysterique. *Archives generales

de medicine,* 1:384–403.

Leary, M., & Kowalski, R. (1990). Impression management: A

   literature review and two component model.

   Psychological Bulletin, 107, 34-37.

Leichner, P., Rallo, J., & Leichner, J. (1989). *A descriptive profile*

   of eating attitudes and behavior among exercising

   women. Montreal, PQ: Unpublished paper from

   Douglass Hospital.

Lindboe, C. & Slettebo, M. (1984). Are your young female

   gymnasts malnourished? *European Journal of Applied*

   Physiology, 52, 457-462.

Ludwig, M. (1996). A sport psychology perspective. *Journal of*

   Physical Education, 67, 31-35.

Mallick, M., Whipple, T., & Huerta, E. (1987). Behavioral and

   psychological traits of weight-conscious teenagers: A

   comparison of eating-disordered patients and high and

   low-risk groups. *Adolescence, 22,* 157-168.

Mangweth B; Pope H., Kemmler G., Ebenbichler C., &

Hausmann, A. (2001). Body image and psychopathology

in male bodybuilders. *Psychotherapy and*

Psychosomatics, 70(1): 38-43.

Marine, R. J. (2000). *Evolution of Survey Modes During the*

1990s. University Park, PA: Unpublished manuscript.

McCormak, S. (2002, August 22). During the height of the roman

empire. *The Daily Bulletin*. Ontario, Canada.

McCreary, D., & Sasse, D. (2000, May). An exploration of the

drive for muscularity in adolescent boys and girls.

Journal of American College Health, 48, 297-304.

McCreary, D., Sasse, D., Saucier, D. M., & Dorsch (2004,

January). Measuring the drive for muscularity: Factorial

validity of the drive for muscularity scale in men and

women. *Psychology of Men and Masculinity, 5*(1), 49-

58.

Mintz, L., & Betz, N. (1986). Prevalence and correlates of eating

   disorder behaviors among undergraduate women.

   Journal of Counseling Psychology, 35, 463-471.

Mitchell, J. (1986). Bulimia: Medical and physiological aspects.

   In *Handbook of Eating Disorders: Physiology,*

   Psychology, and Treatment of Obesity, Anorexia, and

   Bulimia. edited by Brownell and Foreyt. New York: Basic

   Books, Inc.

Monteath, S., & McCabe, M. (1997). The influence of societal

   factors on female body image. *Journal of Social*

   Psychology, 137, 708-727.

Moore, D. (1990). Body image and eating behavior in adolescent

   boys. *American Journal of Diseases in Children, 144,*

   417-432.

Morgan, H. G., & Russell G. F. (1975). Value of family

   background and clinical features as predictors of long-

   term outcome in anorexia nervosa: Four-year follow-up

   study of 41 patients. *Psychological Medicine, 5,* 355-

   371.

Moriarty, D., Moriarty, M. (1994). Eating Disorders and Sports.

Morton R., Phthisiologia seu exercitationes DePhthisi Tribus

Libris Comprehensae. (1689). Reprinted. London, Smith

& Walford, 1994 (cited in Reda M, Sacco G: Anorexia

and the holiness of Saint Catherine of Siena. *Journal of*

Criminal Justice and Popular Culture, 2001; *(8)* 37–47.

Murphy, H. B. (1982). *Comparative psychiatry*. International and

Intercultural Distribution of Mental Illness. Springer,

Berlin.

Natenshon, A. (1999). *When Your Child has an Eating Disorder:*

A Step-by-Step Workbook for Parents and other

Caregivers. San Francisco.

National Collegiate Athletic Association (NCAA). (1991).

Nutrition and Eating Disorders in College Athletics.

Overland Park, KS: NCAA.

Nattiv, A., Agostini R., & Drinkwater B.(1994). The female

athletic triad: The interrelatedness of disordered eating,

amenorrhea, and osteoporosis. *Clinical Sports Medicine,*

13(2), 405-418.

Nattiv, A. & Puffer, J. C. (1991). Lifestyle and health risk of

collegiate athletes. *The Journal of Family Practice, 33*(6):

585-590.

Nelson, W., Hughes, H., Katz, B., & Searlight, H. (1999, Fall).

Anorexic eating attitudes and behaviors of males and

female college students. *Adolescence, 34*(135).

Noles, S., Cash, T., & Winstead, B. (1995). Body image, physical

attractiveness and depression. *Journal of Consulting and*

Clinical Psychology, 53, 88-94.

Norring, C. & Palmer, R. (2005). *EDNOS: Eating disorders not*

otherwise specified: Scientific and clinical perspectives

on the other eating disorders. Psychology Press.

Nudelman, S., Rosen, J.C., & Leitenberg, H. (1988).

Dissimilarities in eating attitudes, body image distortion,

depression and self-esteem between high-intensity

male runners and women with bulimia nervosa.

International Journal of Eating Disorders, 7, 625-635.

O'Connor, P., Lewis, R., & Kirchner, E. (1995). Eating disorder

symptoms in female college gymnasts. *Medicine and*

Science in Sports and Exercise, 550-554.

Oglivie, B.C. (1968). Psychological consistencies within the

personality of high-level competitors. *The Journal of the*

American Medical Association. 205, 156-162.

Orlick, T. (1990). *In pursuit of excellence: How to win sports and*

life through mental training (2nd. Ed.). Champaign, IL:

Leisure Press.

Palmer, R. (2004). Bulimia nervosa: 25 years. *The British Journal*

of Psychiatry. 185: 447-448

Pearce, J. M. (2004). Richard Morton: Origins of anorexia

nervosa. *European Neurology,* 52:191-192

Perry, P. (1986 August-September). Hooked on Perfection.

Verve, 40(42), 79-80.

Person, D., Benson-Quaziena, M., & Rogers, A. (2001, Spring).

Female student athletes and student athletes of color.

New Directions for Student Services, (93).

Petrie, T. (1993). Disordered eating in female collegiate

    gymnasts: Prevalence and personality/attitudinal

    correlates. *Journal of Sport and Exercise Psychology, 15,*

    424-436.

Petrie, T., & Sherman, R. (1999). Recognizing and assisting

    athletes with eating disorders. *Counseling in Sports*

    Medicine, 205-226.

Picard, C. (1999). The level of competition as a factor for the

    development of eating disorders in female collegiate

    athletes. *Journal of Youth and Adolescence, 28,* 583-

    594.

Pierce, E., Daleng, M. & McGowan, R. W. (1993). Scores on

    exercise dependence among dancers. *Journal of*

    Perceptual and Motor Skills. 76, 531-535.

Powers, P., & Johnson, C. (1999). Small victories: Prevention of

    eating disorders among elite athletes. In Piran, N.,

    Levine, M.& Steiner-Adair, C. (Eds.), *Preventing Eating*

    Disorders (pp. 241 - 254). Philadelphia: Taylor & Francis.

Powers, P., Schulman, R., Gleghorn, A., & Prange, M. (1987).

Perceptual and cognitive abnormalities in bulimia.

American Journal of Psychiatry, 144, 1456-1460.

Princeton University Progress Report. Task Force on Health and

Well Being (2004, April). Retrieved on November 27,

2005 from www.princeton.edu/hwbtf.

Prouty, A. M., Protinsky, H. O., & Canady, D. (2002). College

women: Eating behaviors and help-seeking preferences.

Adolescence, 37(146), 353-363.

Rader Programs, *Men and eating disorders:* Retrieved on

October 27, 2005 from

http://www.raderprograms.com/men.aspx

Raphael, F. & Lacey J. (1992). Sociocultural factors in eating

disorders. *Annals of Medicine, 24*, 293-296.

Raudenbush, B., & Zellner, D. (1997). Nobody's satisfied: Effects

of abnormal eating behaviors and actual perceived

weight status and body image satisfaction in males.

Journal of Social and Clinical Psychoogy,16, 95-110.

Reel, J., & Gill, D. (1996). Psychosocial factors related to eating

disorders among high school and college female

cheerleaders. *The Sport Psychologist, 10,* 195-206.

Rhodes, C. (2000). *Life inside the "thin" cage: A personal look*

*into the hidden world of the chronic die*ter. Shaw Books

Ricca, V., Mannucci, E., & Mezzani, B. (2001). Fluoxetine and

fluvoxamine combined with individual cognitive

behavior therapy in binge eating disorders: A one–year

follow-up study. *Psychother Psychosom, 70*(6) 298-306.

Rogers, R. L., & Petrie, T. A. (1996). Personality correlates of

anorexic symptomology in female undergraduates.

Journal of Counseling and Development(75), 138-141.

Rogers, R. L., & Petrie, T. A. (2001). Psychological correlates of

anorexia and bulimic symptomology. *Journal of*

Counseling and Development(79), pp. 178-186.

Root, M. P., Fallon, P, & Friedrich, W. N. (1987). *Bulimia: A*

systems approach to treatment. W. W Norton &

Company Inc.

Rosen, L. & Gross, J. (1987). Prevalence of weight reducing and

weight gaining in adolescent girls and boys. *Health*

Psychology, 6, 131-147.

Rosen, L., & Hough, D. (1988). Pathogenic weight control

behaviors of female college gymnasts. *Journal of Sports*

Medicine, 16, 140-143.

Rosen, L., & McKeag, D. (1986). Pathogenic weight control

behaviors in female athletes. *The Physician and Sports*

Medicine, 14, 79-86.

Rosen, L., Silberg, N. T. & Gross, J. (1988). Eating attitudes test

and eating disorder inventory: Norms for adolescent

girls and boys. *Journal of Consulting and Clinical*

Psychology(56), 305-308.

Ross L., & Gill J. (2002). Eating disorders: Relations with

inconsistent discipline, anxiety, and drinking among

college women. *Psychological Reports, 91*(1), 289-298.

Satmetrix, S. (2001). *Investigating validity in web surveys.*

Retrieved on June 10, 2006 from

http://www.satmetrix.com/public/pdfs/

validity_wp4.pdf

Schneider, J. A., & Agras, W. S. (1987). Bulimia in males: A

matched comparison with females. *International*

Journal of Eating Disorders, 6, 235-242.

Schotte, D., & Stinkard, A. (1987). Bulimia vs. bulimic behaviors

on a college campus. *Journal of American Medical*

Association, 258, 1213–1215.

Schulken, E., Pinciaro, P., Sawyer, R., Jensen, J., & Hoban, M.

(1997). Sorority women's body size perceptions and

their weight related attitudes and behaviors. *Journal of*

American College Health, 46, 69-74.

Schwartz, A. (2006, December 27). *Eating disorders, self*

mutilation and unexpressed emotions: A deadly

relationship. Message posted to www.mentalealth.net

Scott, D. (1988). *Anorexia and bulimia nervosa.* New York

University Press.

Shisslak, C., Crago, M., & Estes, L. (1995). The spectrum of

eating disturbances. *International Journal of Eating*

Disorders, 18(3), 209-219.

Shrout, P. E. (Chair), Hunter, J. E., Harris, R. J., Wilkinson, L.,

Strouss, M. E., Applebaum, M. I., (1996, August).

Significance tests—should they be banned from APA

journals? Symposium conducted at the 104th Annual

Convention of the American Psychologists Association,

Toronto, Canada.

Silverman J. A. (1995): History of anorexia nervosa. In Brownell

K. D., Fairburn C. (Eds.): *Eating Disorders and Obesity. A*

Comprehensive Handbook. New York, The Guilford

Press, 25, 141–144.

Simmonds, M. (1914). Ueber embolische Prozesse inder

hypophysis. *Arch Pathol Anat,* 217, 226–239.

Skolnick, A. (1993). Female athlete triad risk for women. *Journal*

of the American Medical Association, 270, 921-923.

Skowron, E. & Friedlander, M. (1994). Psychological separation, self-control, and weight preoccupation among elite women athletes. *Journal of Counseling and Development, 72*, 3, January-February, 310-315.

Slavin, J. (1987) Eating disorders in athletes. *Journal of Physical Education, Recreation, and Dance, 58*(3).

Slay, H., Hayaki, J., Napolitano, M.A., & Brownell, K. (1998). Motivations for running and eating attitudes in obligatory versus non-obligatory runners. *International Journal of Eating Disorders, 23*, 267-75.

Smith, D. E., Marcus, M.D., Lewis, C. E., Fitzgibbon, M., Schreiner, P. (1998). Prevalence of binge eating disorder, obesity and depression in a biracial cohort of young adults. *Annuls of Behavioral Medicine, 20*, 227-232.

Smolak, L. (1996). *National Eating Disorder Association/Next Door Neighbors Puppet Guide Book.*

Smolak, L., Murnen, S. K., & Ruble, A. E. (2000). Female athletes

and eating problems: A meta-analysis. *International*

Journal of Eating Disorders, 27, 371-380.

Sokol, M., Steinberg, D., Zerbe, K. (1998). Childhood eating

disorders. *Current Opinion Pediatric, 10*(4), 369-377.

Sparks, C. (2005) *Sisterhood of starvation*. iMPrint Magazine

(on-line).

Story, M., Rosenwinkel, K., Himes, J., Resnick, M., Harris, L., &

Blum, R. (1991). Demographic and risk factors

associated with chronic dieting in adolescents.

American Journal of Diseases of Children, 145, 994-998.

Stoutjesdyk, D., & Jevne, R. (1993). Eating disorders among high

performance athletes. *Journal of Youth and*

Adolescence, 22,(3), 271.

Striegel-Moore, R. H., Silberstein, L. R., & Rodin, J. (1986).

Toward an understanding of risk factors for bulimia.

American Psychologist, 41, 246-263

Striegel-Moore, R. H. & Smolak, L. (2000). The influence of

ethnicity on eating disorders in women. In Eisler, R. M.,

& Hersen, M. (eds.). *Handbook of Gender, Culture, and*

Health. Mahwah, NJ: Lawrence Erlbaum Associates,

227-253.

Strumia, R., Manzato, E., & Gualandi, M. (2003). Cutaneous

Manifestations in Male anorexia nervosa: Four cases.

Acta Dermato-Venereologica, 83(6), 464-465.

Sundgot- Borgen, J. (1994a). Eating disorders in female athletes.

Sports Medicine, 17, 176-188.

Sundgot-Borgen, J. (1994b). Risk and trigger factors for the

development of eating disorders in female elite

athletes. *Medicine and Science in Sports and Exercise,*

414-418.

Sundgot-Borgen, J. (1999). Eating disorders among male and

female elite athletes. *British Journal of Sports Medicine,*

33(6), 434.

Taub, D., & Blinde, E. (1992). Eating disorders among adolescent

female athletes: Influence of athletic participation and

sport team membership. *Adolescence, 27*, 883-848.

Terry, P. C., Lane, A. M., Lane, H. J. & Keohane, L. (1999).

Development and validation of a mood measure for

adolescents. *Journal of Sports Sciences (117),* 861-872.

The *Renfrew Center Foundation for Eating Disorders. Eating*

disorder 101 Guide: A Summary of Issues, Statistics and

Resources. Retrieved on September 19, 2002 from

http://www.refrew.org

The Renfrew Center Foundation: Advancing the Education,

Prevention, Research & Treatment of Eating Disorders.

Retrieve on November 13, 2004 from

http://www.renfrew.org/research.asp

Thiel, A., Gottfried, H., Hesse, F. (1993). Body image of the male

athlete: A study of the psychological health of wrestlers

and rowers of the lower weight class. *Psychotherapy,*

Psychosomatic, Medizinische Psychology, 43, 432-438.

Thiel, A., Gottfried, H., Hesse, F. (1993). Sub-clinical eating

   disorders in male athletes: A study of the low weight

   category in rowers and wrestlers. *Acta Psychiatrica*

   Scandinavica, 88, 259-265.

Thompson, J. K. (1999). *Exacting beauty: Theory, assessment,*

   and treatment of body image disturbance. American

   Psychological Association.

Thompson, J. K, Covert, M., Stormer, S. (1999). Body image,

   social comparison, and eating disturbance: A covariance

   structure modeling investigation. *International Journal*

   of Eating Disorders, 26(1), May, 43-51.

Thompson, Ron. Personal electronic communication, May 8,

   2006.

Thompson, R. & Sherman, R. (1993) Helping athletes with eating

   disorders. *Human Kinetics.* Champaign IL.

Thompson, R., & Sherman, R. (1999). "Good athlete" traits and

   characteristics of anorexia nervosa: Are they similar?

   Eating Disorders: The Journal of Treatment &

   Prevention, 7(3), 181-190.

Thornton, B., Leo, R., & Alberg, K. (1991). Gender role typing, the superwoman ideal, and the potential for eating disorders. *Sex Roles, 25*, 469-484.

Thornton, E. W., & Scott, S. E. (1995). Motivation in the committed runner: Correlations between self-report scales and behaviour. *Health Promotion International, 10*, 177-184.

Upcraft, M. L., & Wortman, T. I. (2000, Fall). Web-based Data Collection and Assessment in Student Affairs. *Student Affairs On-Line, 1*(3).

Veal, D. (1995). Does primary exercise dependence really exist? In: Exercise addiction: Motivation for participation in sport and exercise. *British Psychological Society.*

Velez, L. Regurgitated The Mexican Spitfire in an American Vomitorium William Anthony Nericcio. From http://literature.sdsu.edu/textmex/NOVvelez.pdf

Vitousek, K., Watson, S., & Wilson, G. (1998). Enhancing motivation for change in treatment-resistant eating disorders. *Clinical Psychology Review, 18(4)*, 391-420.

Wang, M., Yesalis, C., Fitzhugh, E., Buckley, W., & Smiciklas-

    Wright, H. (1994). Desire for weight gain and potential

    risks of adolescent males using anabolic steroids.

    Perceptual and Motor Skills, 78, 267-274.

Wantland, D. J., Portillo, C. J., Holzemer, W. L., Slaughter, R. &

    McGhee, E. M. (2004, November). The effectiveness of

    web-based vs. non-web-based interventions: A meta-

    analysis of behavioral change outcomes. *Journal of*

    Medical Internet Research(10)6.

Wittig, A. F., & Schurr, K. T. (1994). Psychological characteristics

    of women volleyball players: Relationships with injuries,

    rehabilitation, and team success. *Personality and Social*

    Psychology Bulletin, 20, 322-330.

Williamson, D. A., Netemeyer, R. G., Jackman, L. P., Anderson,

    D. A., Funsch, C. L. & Rabalais, J. Y. (1995). Structural

    equation modeling of risk factors for the development

    of eating disorder symptoms in female athletes.

    International Journal of Eating Disorders. 17, 387-393.

Woodside, D., Bulik, C., Thornton, L., Klump, K. Tozzi, F., Fichter,

M, Halmi, K, Kaplan, A, Strober, M, & Devlin, B.

Personality in men with eating disorders. *Journal of*

Psychosomatic Research. 57. 3, p. 273-278.

World Wide Charter for Action on Eating Disorders. Retrieved

on November 12, 2005 from

http://aedweb.org/PressConference/

Charter_History.pdf

Yates, A. (1991). *Compulsive exercise and the eating disorders.*

New York: Brunner/Mazel.

Yates, A., Leehey. K. & Shisslak, C. (1983). Running: An analogue

of anorexia? *New England Journal of Medicine, 308,*

251-255.

Yeager, K., Agostini, R., Nattiv, A., & Drinkwater, B. (1993). The

female athlete triad: Disordered eating, amenorrhea,

osteoporosis. *Medicine and Science in Sports and*

Exercise, 25, 775-777.

Zerbe, K. J. (1993). The body betrayed: Women, eating

disorders, and the overtraining syndrome. In W.F. Epling

& W. D. Pierce (Eds.), *Activity anorexia: Theory,*

research, and treatment (pp. 197 - 188). Mahwah, NJ:

Lawrence Erlbaum Associates.

Ziegler, P., & San Khoo, C. (1998). Body image and dieting

behaviors among elite figure skaters. *International*

Journal of Eating Disorders, 24, 421-427.

www.ingramcontent.com/pod-product-compliance
Lightning Source LLC
Chambersburg PA
CBHW060612290526
45793CB00001B/7